THE BILL OF RIGHTS

INTERPRETING PRIMARY DOCUMENTS

Tom Head, Book Editor

Daniel Leone, President
Bonnie Szumski, Publisher
Scott Barbour, Managing Editor

**GREENHAVEN
PRESS®**

THOMSON
™
GALE

San Diego • Detroit • New York • San Francisco • Cleveland
New Haven, Conn. • Waterville, Maine • London • Munich

Acknowledgments

Tom Head extends special thanks to managing editor Scott Barbour and production editor Lisa Mitchell. Charlie Brenner of the Jackson/Hinds Library System, Sherry Stroup of Kessler-Hancock Information Services, and Shane Hunt of 4ResearchSolutions.com all played an instrumental role in helping to locate hard-to-find research materials. As always, Tom would also like to thank his family for their love and support.

LIBRARY OF CONGRESS CATALOGING-IN-PUBLICATION DATA

The Bill of Rights / Tom Head, book editor.
    p. cm. — (Interpreting primary documents)
Includes bibliographical references and index.
ISBN 0-7377-1081-0 (pbk. : alk. paper) — ISBN 0-7377-1082-9 (lib. : alk. paper)
    1. United States. Constitution. 1st–10th Amendments.—Sources. 2. Civil rights—United States—History—Sources. I. Head, Tom. II. Series.
KF4744 2004
342.73'085—dc21   2003051616

Printed in the United States of America

CONTENTS

Chapter 4: A Well-Regulated Militia

Chapter 5: Rights of the Accused

to British customs officers. These concerns were
later incorporated into the Fourth Amendment.

FOREWORD

In a debate on the nature of the historian's task, the Canadian intellectual Michael Ignatieff wrote, "I don't think history is a lesson in patriotism. It should be a lesson in truth. And the truth is both painful and many-sided." Part of Ignatieff's point was that those who seek to understand the past should guard against letting prejudice or patriotism interfere with the truth. This point, although simple, is subtle. Everyone would agree that patriotism is no excuse for outright fabrication, and that prejudice should never induce a historian to deliberately lie or deceive. Ignatieff's concern, however, was not so much with deliberate falsification as it was with the way prejudice and patriotism can lead to selective perception, which can skew the judgment of even those who are sincere in their efforts to understand the past. The truth, especially about the how and why of historical events, is seldom simple, and those who wish to genuinely understand the past must be sensitive to its complexities.

Each of the anthologies in the Greenhaven Press Interpreting Primary Documents series strives to portray the events and attitudes of the past in all their complexity. Rather than providing a simple narrative of the events, each volume presents a variety of views on the issues and events under discussion and encourages the student to confront and examine the complexity that attends the genuine study of history.

Furthermore, instead of aiming simply to transmit information from historian to student, the series is designed to develop and train students to become historians themselves, by focusing on the interpretation of primary documents. Such documents, including newspaper articles, speeches, personal reflections, letters, diaries, memoranda, and official reports, are the raw material from which the historian refines an authentic understanding of the past. The anthology examining desegregation, for instance, includes the voices of presidents, state governors, and ordinary citizens, and draws from the *Congressional Record,* newspapers and magazines, letters, and books published at the time. The selections differ in scope and opinion as well, allowing the student to examine the issue of desegregation from a variety of perspectives. By looking frankly at the arguments offered by those in favor of racial segregation and by those opposed, for example, students can better understand those arguments, the people who advanced them, and the time in which they lived.

The structure of each book in the Interpreting Primary Documents series helps readers sharpen the critical faculties the serious study of history requires. A concise introduction outlines the era or event at hand and provides the necessary historical background. The chapters themselves begin with a preface containing a straightforward account of the events discussed and an overview of how these events can be interpreted in different ways by examining the different documents in the chapter. The selections, in turn, are chosen for their accessibility and relevance, and each is preceded by a short introduction offering historical context and a summary of the author's point of view. A set of questions to guide interpretation accompanies each article and encourages readers to examine the authors' prejudices, probe their assumptions, and compare and contrast the various perspectives offered in the chapter. Finally, a detailed timeline traces the development of key events, a comprehensive bibliography of selected secondary material guides further research, and a thorough index lets the reader quickly access relevant information.

As Ignatieff remarked, in the same debate in which he urged the historian to favor truth over blind patriotism, "History for me is the study of arguments." The Interpreting Primary Documents series is for readers eager to understand the arguments, and attitudes, that animated historical change.

The Bill of Rights

The Bill of Rights was originally passed by Congress as an almost useless compromise, an unenforceable legislative statement of principles drafted to appease a small number of hard-to-please politicians and activists. As the Supreme Court became its guardian, it became an essential guiding document in federal law. Following the Civil War, its power was expanded further to protect individual rights against violations by state laws. Over time, the Bill of Rights has slowly grown to become the most central and widely cited document in the American legal system.

Ancestors of the U.S. Bill of Rights

The American concept of a bill of rights can be traced to England. In the Magna Carta of 1215 and the English Bill of Rights of 1689, the British government ceded basic rights to some of its citizens and, in so doing, restricted its own power to write and enforce laws. The Magna Carta came about under the rule of England's King John (1167–1216), generally regarded as one of the most wicked kings ever to take the English throne. John rose to power upon the death of his older brother King Richard I ("Richard the Lion-Hearted") (1157–1199), whom he had tried to overthrow five years before. When the despised and politically feeble King John began to tax England's barons, they led a military revolt against him. He quickly surrendered and agreed to sign a document ceding over some basic rights to freemen and limiting his own authority to make laws. Although the Magna Carta did not guarantee the sort of basic rights that are associated with rights declarations today, it established a basic code of criminal justice and made the king subject to his barons on some matters, such as tax law.

More sweeping was the English Bill of Rights (1689), which came about following the Glorious Revolution of 1688. King James II (1633–1701) was a Roman Catholic king at a time when Roman Catholicism was both unpopular and restricted by law in England. Due to his pro-Catholic policies and his disregard for Parliament, James was deposed following a bloodless coup. An English bill of rights was drafted that both limited the king's ability to overrule Parliament and guaranteed some rights to Protestants, including free speech in Parliament, the right to petition the king, and certain legal rights (such as the prohibition against cruel and unusual punishment). The English Bill of Rights of 1689 is not impressive by contemporary standards (as it promotes religious discrimination), but it did establish a basic structure for rights declarations upon which the bills of rights of both the United States and France are loosely based.

Legislator George Mason (1725–1792) first brought the idea of a bill of rights to America when he proposed the Virginia Declaration of Rights of 1776. This document both challenged the authority of British colonial rule and established a precedent for the Bill of Rights by guaranteeing personal rights to free speech and religious liberty. The declaration begins:

> That all men are by nature free and independent, and have certain inherent rights, of which, when they enter into a state of society, they cannot, by any compact, deprive or divest their posterity; namely, the enjoyment of life and liberty, with the means of acquiring and possessing property, and pursuing and obtaining happiness and safety.[1]

The language of the Virginia declaration would inspire Thomas Jefferson (1743–1826) to draft a national declaration of independence later the same year. Jefferson's declaration held "to be self-evident, that all men are created equal, that they are endowed by their Creator with certain unalienable Rights, that among these are Life, Liberty and the pursuit of Happiness."[2] By the time of the American Revolution, the American cause had been inextricably linked to the idea that all citizens possess basic rights, whether those rights are granted by their respective governments or not.

The First Constitutional Amendments

When the original Articles of Confederation were drafted in 1777, a bill of rights was considered unnecessary. The U.S. government was an alliance of independent states rather than a single national government. Because the national government had no power to restrict people's rights, there was no perceived need for laws to prevent it from doing so. During the Constitutional Convention of 1787, which was assembled to create a more permanent set of resolutions defining the powers of the national government, the idea of adding a bill of rights to the Constitution was raised but quickly voted down. The document was passed without a bill of rights.

When the Constitution was sent to the states for ratification, however, a debate broke out between the Federalists, who supported a strong national government, and the Anti-Federalists, who supported retaining the spirit of the Articles of Confederation. The greatest single concern of the Anti-Federalist movement was that the national government would become tyrannical. In an effort to prevent such an outcome, the Anti-Federalists suggested incorporating a bill of rights into the U.S. Constitution. Meanwhile, most Federalists objected to a bill of rights on the grounds that it was unnecessary. They argued that the Constitution reserved only a few specific powers to the U.S. government in the first place. Those that were not reserved to the government were automatically reserved to the people under the doctrine of natural law. This doctrine holds that basic rights such as life, liberty, and property belong to the people. Many Federalists believed that, besides being unnecessary, a bill of rights would be dangerous. If the national government had the power to delineate which individual rights to protect, they reasoned, it could presume to decide which rights to limit.

Although the Constitution passed without a bill of rights, some Anti-Federalists felt that it would be worthwhile to specifically protect through constitutional amendments such individual rights as free speech, religious exercise, and jury trials. Some supporters of the Constitution, such as Thomas Jefferson, were inclined to sympathize with the Anti-Federalists on this point. In a 1789 letter to James Madison (1751–1836), nicknamed the father of the Constitution for his work in getting the document written and passed, Thomas Jefferson urged the passage of a bill of rights:

> The Declaration of rights is like all other human blessings alloyed with some inconveniences, and not accomplishing fully its object. But the good in this instance vastly overweighs the evil. . . . The inconveniences of the Declaration are that it may cramp government in its useful exertions. But the evil of this is shortlived, moderate, [and] reparable. The inconveniences of the want of a Declaration are permanent, afflicting, [and] irreparable: they are in constant progression from bad to worse.[3]

Madison submitted a draft of his proposed bill of rights several months later, and Congress passed its modified version by the end of the year. After ratification by the states, the final Bill of Rights consisted of ten amendments that covered a wide range of topics, guaranteeing citizens individual rights such as freedom of speech and religious liberty and protecting them from excessive bail, unwarranted searches, and cruel and unusual punishment. Madison was able to respond to earlier Federalist concerns about unspecified rights by way of the Ninth and Tenth Amendments (which reserve all unspecified rights to the states and to the people). However, one serious problem still remained: Although the Bill of Rights was a comprehensive statement of human rights, it was virtually impossible to enforce. The judiciary was typically called on to interpret law, but it had not yet established its role as protector of the Bill of Rights. It would take decades of Supreme Court rulings and an additional amendment—the fourteenth—before the Bill of Rights would become the powerful document it is today.

The Supreme Court Stakes Its Claim

The practical ineffectiveness of the Bill of Rights had become evident as early as the end of the eighteenth century. In 1798, responding to internal criticism from the new Democratic-Republican Party and political disagreement with France, the U.S. Congress passed the Alien and Sedition Acts. These acts allowed the U.S. government to deport any resident alien at will and to arrest anyone for making false statements against public figures. In response, the state legislatures of Virginia and Kentucky passed resolutions condemning the unpopular legislation as unconstitutional on the basis that it violated both the First Amendment (protecting free speech) and the Ninth Amendment (protecting state's rights), but the legislatures were powerless to change the law. All of the acts had either expired or been repealed by 1802, but it had become clear to some that a mechanism for challenging unconstitutional legislation was needed.

In 1803 the Supreme Court took its first step in establishing itself as the interpreter of the Bill of Rights. When President John Adams (1735–1826) left office in March 1801, he had appointed James Marbury and three other judges to federal office. The new president, Thomas Jefferson, declared the appointments null and void because they had not been made official by sundown. Marbury sued Jefferson's secretary of state, James Madison, under the Judiciary Act of 1789. The Judiciary Act gave the Supreme Court power to issue writs of mandamus (mandate), ordering American citizens to perform a given duty. The Supreme Court was placed in a position in which, regardless of outcome, it would expand its own power: Either it could force the secretary of state to approve the appointment of a judge, or it could strike down the Judiciary Act as unconstitutional. In *Marbury v. Madison* (1803) the Court chose to do the latter, and in so doing established judicial review—the principle by which the Supreme Court strikes down unconstitutional legislation. By giving itself the power to strike down legislation for violating the Constitution proper, the Supreme Court also established its role as the institution responsible for striking down laws that violated the Bill of Rights. As Chief Justice John Marshall wrote in his majority opinion:

> It is apparent, that the framers of the Constitution contemplated that instrument as a rule for the government of courts, as well as of the legislature. Why otherwise does it direct the judges to take an oath to support it? . . . The particular phraseology of the Constitution of the United States confirms and strengthens the principle, supposed to be essential to all written constitutions, that a law repugnant to the constitution is void; and that courts, as well as other departments, are bound by that instrument.[4]

Under John Marshall, the Supreme Court became known as the body responsible for interpreting the Bill of Rights and thereby determining whether or not a given piece of federal legislation violates it.

The Fourteenth Amendment

Although *Marbury v. Madison* established the Supreme Court as the enforcer of the Bill of Rights, the ruling applied only to federal law. State laws remained beyond the purview of the Bill of Rights. When James Madison proposed a bill of rights in 1789, he had originally included a clause stipulating that "no state shall violate the equal rights of conscience, or the freedom of the press, or the trial by jury in criminal cases."[5] At some point after Madison's proposal passed in the House—but before it came up for a Senate vote—the language was quietly removed, and did not appear in the final version of the Bill of Rights. Any ambiguous state law jurisdiction for the Bill of Rights was swept away in *Barron v. Baltimore* (1833), when the U.S. Supreme Court formally ruled that the Bill of Rights had no jurisdiction over state legislatures.

The key to applying the Bill of Rights to state law would be the Fourteenth Amendment, passed after the Civil War. In the wake of the war, many southern governments passed "black codes" directed against African Americans in general and former slaves in particular. These codes included curfews, work documentation requirements, and other abridgments of legal rights, forcing black southerners to live under circumstances that differed as little as possible from slavery itself. Primarily in an effort to defeat these laws, Congress passed the Fourteenth Amendment in 1866. Section I specifically holds states accountable for preserving human rights:

> All persons born or naturalized in the United States, and subject to the jurisdiction thereof, are citizens of the United States and of the State wherein they reside. No State shall make or enforce any law which shall abridge the privileges or immunities of citizens of the United States; nor shall any State deprive any person of life, liberty, or property, without due process of law; nor deny to any person within its jurisdiction the equal protection of the laws. [6]

For almost six decades, this section was interpreted as a broad defense against particularly inhumane laws—not as an affirmation of the Bill of Rights per se. This changed in *Gitlow v. New York* (1925), when the Supreme Court upheld the conviction of an American Socialist who had written politically incendiary material. While evaluating the

New York law as part of his majority ruling, Justice Edward T. Sanford made an assumption that had not previously been made: "The 'liberty' protected by the Fourteenth Amendment includes the liberty of speech and of the press."[7] With these sixteen words, Sanford inaugurated the "incorporation doctrine," which holds that the Fourteenth Amendment expands the authority of the Bill of Rights to include state law. In its 136-year history, the Bill of Rights had gone from being an unenforceable federal legislative statement of principles to a powerful legal code in its own right, enforced by the Supreme Court against both state and federal encroachments on individual liberties.

The Bill of Rights Today

The success of the Bill of Rights has been gradual and hard-won. Over the past century, the Supreme Court has refined the way it interprets the Bill of Rights. Interpretations now tend to be highly complex and rely on a vast tradition of judicial standards that are used to interpret the broad language of the Constitution in a more narrow and specific way. In this respect, the Bill of Rights is a "living document": The way it has been interpreted has changed over time, and will continue to change over time.

Today's standards might seem strange to an earlier Court. Some old laws, such as the Sedition Act of 1918 (which criminalized speech advocating revolution), survived under last century's standards but would clearly be declared unconstitutional under the free speech guidelines accepted by even the most conservative justices on the contemporary Court. Public school prayer, once regarded as commonplace, can no longer be officially sanctioned by teachers and education administrators under the Court's modern rulings on the separation of church and state. And the right to privacy—which is not explicitly given in the Constitution but can be inferred from the Fourth Amendment (which protects citizens' "right to be secure in their persons, houses, papers, and effects") and Ninth Amendment (which reserves unspecified rights to the people)—has played a major role in recent rulings on a number of controversial social issues, ranging from abortion to homosexuality.

Although the Bill of Rights protects a wide variety of rights, several have been the topic of particularly divisive debate since its inception. For purposes of this book, we have chosen to focus on the most fiercely debated amendments: the first, second, fourth, and fifth, which deal with the freedom of speech, religious liberty, the right to bear arms, and rights of the accused. These debates have produced a great number of engaging primary documents by well-known American historical figures.

Notes
1. Virginia Declaration of Rights, 1776.
2. United States Declaration of Independence, 1776.
3. Thomas Jefferson, letter to James Madison, March 15, 1789.
4. Chief Justice John Marshall, majority opinion in *Marbury v. Madison* (1803).
5. James Madison, Proposed Amendments to the Constitution, June 8, 1789.
6. Fourteenth Amendment to the Constitution, 1866.
7. Justice Edward T. Sanford, majority opinion in *Gitlow v. New York* (1925).

AMENDING THE CONSTITUTION

CHAPTER PREFACE

When the Constitutional Convention met in 1787 to write a replacement for the Articles of Confederation, two schools of thought were represented. The Federalists, who supported a strong national government, wished to see a fairly comprehensive constitution stating the rights and authority of the national government. The Anti-Federalists, who supported strong state governments linked by an alliance, wished to preserve the spirit of the Articles of Confederation and thereby opposed the new Constitution.

By the time the Constitutional Convention had assembled, numerous states had already passed bills of rights. The Virginia Declaration of Rights, the Declaration of Rights of the Commonwealth of Massachusetts, and the Northwest Ordinance all guaranteed basic rights to state citizens. The Anti-Federalists noticed that no such guarantees existed in the new national Constitution and feared that a strong national government might one day oppress citizens of the independent United States, much as the British government had oppressed the colonists. The call for a bill of rights was also an effective stalling tactic. By drawing the debate into a discussion of abstract rights, the Anti-Federalists could slow down the constitutional ratification process and preserve the strong state governments created by the Articles of Confederation.

Although some Federalists (such as Thomas Jefferson) sympathized with the call for a national bill of rights, their main priority was to get a national constitution passed. They succeeded at this goal, but not without dissent. Numerous high-profile American political thinkers, such as George Mason, opposed the new Constitution because it lacked a bill of rights.

Once the Constitution was passed, a few influential Federalists united with Anti-Federalists to support national amendments constituting a bill of rights. In 1789 James Madison—one of those Federalists who had rejected the idea of a bill of rights two years earlier—led the call to add ten amendments to the U.S. Constitution guaranteeing basic rights to the individual states and their citizens.

Opposition to a bill of rights had largely vanished by 1789, but the Federalist-controlled Congress was not particularly enthusiastic about what was widely perceived to be an Anti-Federalist concern. It took nearly four months—from May to September—for the House and the Senate to approve final wording for a bill of rights, and it took another two years for its ratification.

The readings in this chapter represent the bill of rights debate as it existed in the late 1780s.

Predecessors to the U.S. Bill of Rights

Part I: The English Parliament; Part II: George Mason

Although the U.S. Bill of Rights was the most radically libertarian federal document of its time, its basic goal—to protect citizens by prohibiting a government from passing certain laws—was not a new one. The English tradition of protecting citizens from government abuse dated back to the Magna Carta of 1215, which gave English citizens some basic rights in dealing with their government. The two documents that most directly influenced the Bill of Rights were the English Bill of Rights (1689) and the Virginia Declaration of Rights (1776).

The English Bill of Rights excerpted in Part I was passed after the short and turbulent reign of King James II (1685–1688). James was extremely unpopular even before he became king because he was a Catholic at a time when anti-Catholic sentiment in the country was extremely fierce (Catholics were not permitted to hold office in Parliament, for example). Taking on powers that had originally belonged to Parliament, James stacked England's highest court with his own supporters and repealed legislation without due process. In what was called the Glorious Revolution of 1688, James's Protestant son-in-law—King William of Orange—ascended the throne, and James escaped to France. In an effort to secure Parliament's role in determining English policy, William and the Parliament agreed to the English Bill of Rights, which granted considerable rights to Parliament and English Protestants. Although radically different from the U.S. Bill of Rights in function, it provided a basic structure upon which later rights declarations were based.

Part I: *The English Bill of Rights*, 1689. Part II: *The Virginia Declaration of Rights*, 1776.

The Virginia Declaration of Rights, excerpted in Part II, was the brainchild of George Mason (1725–1792), a rich Virginia planter who was dedicated to the concept of natural rights. Although similar documents, such as the Massachusetts Declaration of Rights (1780) and the Northwest Ordinance (1787), played influential roles as well, it is Mason's declaration that is generally credited as the primary model for the U.S. Bill of Rights. The Virginia Declaration of Rights also influenced another important historical document: Thomas Jefferson's Declaration of Independence, written later in the same year.

As you read, consider the following questions:
1. What actions of the monarchy does the English Bill of Rights outlaw?
2. According to Mason, what is the primary purpose of government?

I

Whereas the late King James the Second, by the assistance of divers evil counsellors, judges and ministers employed by him, did endeavour to subvert and extirpate the Protestant religion and the laws and liberties of this kingdom. . . .

And whereas the said late King James the Second having abdicated the government and the throne being thereby vacant, his Highness the prince of Orange (whom it hath pleased Almighty God to make the glorious instrument of delivering this kingdom from popery and arbitrary power) did (by the advice of the Lords Spiritual and Temporal and divers principal persons of the Commons) cause letters to be written to the Lords Spiritual and Temporal being Protestants, and other letters to the several counties, cities, universities, boroughs and cinque ports, for the choosing of such persons to represent them as were of right to be sent to Parliament, to meet and sit at Westminster upon the two and twentieth day of January in this year one thousand six hundred eighty and eight [old style date], in order to such an establishment as that their religion, laws and liberties might not again be in danger of being subverted, upon which letters elections having been accordingly made;

Rights and Liberties

And thereupon the said Lords Spiritual and Temporal and Commons, pursuant to their respective letters and elections, being now assembled in a full and free representative of this nation, taking into their most serious consideration the best means for attaining the ends aforesaid, do in the first place (as their ancestors in like case have usually done) for the vindicating and asserting their ancient rights and liberties declare

That the pretended power of suspending the laws or the execution of laws by regal authority without consent of Parliament is illegal;

That the pretended power of dispensing with laws or the execution of laws by regal authority, as it hath been assumed and exercised of late, is illegal;

That the commission for erecting the late Court of Commissioners for Ecclesiastical Causes, and all other commissions and courts of like nature, are illegal and pernicious;

That levying money for or to the use of the Crown by pretence of prerogative, without grant of Parliament, for longer time, or in other manner than the same is or shall be granted, is illegal;

That it is the right of the subjects to petition the king, and all commitments and prosecutions for such petitioning are illegal;

That the raising or keeping a standing army within the kingdom in time of peace, unless it be with consent of Parliament, is against law;

That the subjects which are Protestants may have arms for their defence suitable to their conditions and as allowed by law;

That election of members of Parliament ought to be free;

That the freedom of speech and debates or proceedings in Parliament ought not to be impeached or questioned in any court or place out of Parliament;

That excessive bail ought not to be required, nor excessive fines imposed, nor cruel and unusual punishments inflicted;

That jurors ought to be duly impanelled and returned, and jurors which pass upon men in trials for high treason ought to be freeholders;

That all grants and promises of fines and forfeitures of particular persons before conviction are illegal and void;

And that for redress of all grievances, and for the amending, strengthening and preserving of the laws, Parliaments ought to be held frequently.

King and Parliament

And they do claim, demand and insist upon all and singular the premises as their undoubted rights and liberties, and that no declarations, judgments, doings or proceedings to the prejudice of the people in any of the said premises ought in any wise to be drawn hereafter into consequence or example; to which demand of their rights they are particularly encouraged by the declaration of his Highness the prince of Orange as being the only means for obtaining a full redress and remedy therein. Having therefore an entire confidence that his said Highness the prince of Orange will perfect the deliverance so far advanced by him, and will still preserve them from the violation of their rights which they have here asserted, and from all other attempts upon their religion, rights and liberties, the said Lords Spiritual and Temporal and Commons assembled at Westminster do resolve that William and Mary, prince and princess of Orange, be and be declared king and queen of England, France and Ireland and the dominions thereunto belonging, to hold the crown and royal dignity of the said kingdoms and dominions to them, the said prince and princess, during their lives and the life of the survivor to them, and that the sole and full exercise of the regal power be only in and executed by the said prince of Orange in the names of the said prince and princess during their joint lives, and after their deceases the said crown and royal dignity of the same kingdoms and dominions to be to the heirs of the body of the said princess, and for default of such issue to the heirs of the body of the said prince of Orange. And the Lords Spiritual and Temporal and Commons do pray the said prince and princess to accept the same accordingly. . . .

And be it further declared and enacted by the authority aforesaid, that from and after this present session of Parliament no dispensation by non obstante of or to any statute or any part thereof shall be allowed, but that the same shall be held void and of no effect, except a dispensation be allowed of in such statute, and except in such cases as shall be specially provided for by one or more bill or bills to be passed during this present session of Parliament.

Provided that no charter or grant or pardon granted before the three and twentieth day of October in the year of our Lord one thousand six hundred eighty-nine shall be any ways impeached or invalidated by this Act, but that the same shall be and remain of the same force and effect in law and no other than as if this Act had never been made.

II

I. That all men are by nature equally free and independent, and have certain inherent rights, of which, when they enter into a state of society, they cannot, by any compact, deprive or divest their posterity; namely, the enjoyment of life and liberty, with the means of acquiring and possessing property, and pursuing and obtaining happiness and safety.

II. That all power is vested in, and consequently derived from, the people; that magistrates are their trustees and servants, and at all times amenable to them.

III. That government is, or ought to be, instituted for the common benefit, protection, and security of the people, nation or community; of all the various modes and forms of government that is best, which is capable of producing the greatest degree of happiness and safety and is most effectually secured against the danger of maladministration; and that, whenever any government shall be found inadequate or contrary to these purposes, a majority of the community hath an indubitable, unalienable, and indefeasible right to reform, alter or abolish it, in such manner as shall be judged most conducive to the public weal.

IV. That no man, or set of men, are entitled to exclusive or separate emoluments or privileges from the community, but in consideration of public services; which, not being descendible, neither ought the offices of magistrate, legislator, or judge be hereditary.

V. That the legislative and executive powers of the state should be separate and distinct from the judicative; and, that the members of the two first may be restrained from oppression by feeling and participating the burthens of the people, they should, at fixed periods, be reduced to a private station, return into that body from which they were originally taken, and the vacancies be supplied by frequent, certain, and regular elections in which all, or any part of the former members, to be again eligible, or ineligible, as the laws shall direct.

VI. That elections of members to serve as representatives of the people in assembly ought to be free; and that all men, having sufficient evidence of permanent common interest with, and attachment to, the community have the right of suffrage and cannot be taxed or deprived of their property for public uses without their own consent or that of their representatives so elected, nor bound by any law to which they have not, in like manner, assented, for the public good.

VII. That all power of suspending laws, or the execution of laws, by any authority without consent of the representatives of the people is injurious to their rights and ought not to be exercised.

VIII. That in all capital or criminal prosecutions a man hath a right to demand the cause and nature of his accusation to be confronted with the accusers and witnesses, to call for evidence in his favor, and to a speedy trial by an impartial jury of his vicinage, without whose unanimous consent he cannot be found guilty, nor can he be compelled to give evidence against himself; that no man be deprived of his liberty except by the law of the land or the judgement of his peers.

IX. That excessive bail ought not to be required, nor excessive fines imposed; nor cruel and unusual punishments inflicted.

X. That general warrants, whereby any officer or messenger may be commanded to search suspected places without evidence of a fact committed, or to seize any person or persons not named, or whose offense is not particularly described and supported by evidence, are grievous and oppressive and ought not to be granted.

XI. That in controversies respecting property and in suits between man and man, the ancient trial by jury is preferable to any other and ought to be held sacred.

XII. That the freedom of the press is one of the greatest bulwarks of liberty and can never be restrained but by despotic governments.

XIII. That a well regulated militia, composed of the body of the people, trained to arms, is the proper, natural, and safe defense of a free state; that standing armies, in time of peace, should be avoided as dangerous to liberty; and that, in all cases, the military should be under strict subordination to, and be governed by, the civil power.

XIV. That the people have a right to uniform government; and therefore, that no government separate from, or independent of, the government of Virginia, ought to be erected or established within the limits thereof.

XV. That no free government, or the blessings of liberty, can be preserved to any people but by a firm adherence to justice, moderation, temperance, frugality, and virtue and by frequent recurrence to fundamental principles.

XVI. That religion, or the duty which we owe to our Creator and the manner of discharging it, can be directed by reason and conviction, not by force or violence; and therefore, all men are equally entitled to the free exercise of religion, according to the dictates of conscience; and that it is the mutual duty of all to practice Christian forbearance, love, and charity toward each other.

A Bill of Rights Would Be Absurd

Noah Webster

When Noah Webster (1758–1843) published his first spelling book in 1782, he discovered that there was no American copyright standard. After traveling to all thirteen state capitals in an effort to establish such a standard, he saw a need for a strong national government and became one of the decade's leading Federalists.

In this 1787 article, Webster defends the original Constitution from critics who wish to attach a bill of rights to it. He describes the concept of a rights contract as "absurd." Although bills of rights make sense under a monarchy, in which the rights of the people need to be protected from encroachment by the king or queen, Webster argues they are unnecessary in a system of representative democracy. Furthermore, he contends that a bill of rights would be unenforceable (since a government can change its own laws at any time) and contrary to the spirit of democracy (as it constitutes prior restriction of self-government).

Webster's patriotism did not dim with the passage of the Bill of Rights. He remained a vocal defender of American culture, and it was in service of that culture that he published his first *American Dictionary* in 1828.

As you read, consider the following questions:
1. What lesson does Webster draw from the William Pitt affair?
2. According to Webster, whose rights did the Magna Carta protect?

Giles Hickory (Noah Webster), "On the Absurdity of a Bill of Rights," *American Magazine*, December 1787.

One of the principal objections to the new Federal Constitution is, that it contains no *Bill of Rights*. This objection, I presume to assert, is founded on ideas of government that are totally false. Men seem determined to adhere to old prejudices, and reason *wrong*, because our ancestors reasoned *right*. A Bill of Rights against the encroachments of Kings and Barons, or against any power independent of the people, is perfectly intelligible; but a Bill of Rights against the encroachments of an elective Legislature, that is, against our *own* encroachments on *ourselves*, is a curiosity in government.

The Concept of Rights in England

One half the people who read books, have so little ability to apply what they read to their own practice, that they had better not read at all. The English nation, from which we descended, have been gaining their liberties, inch by inch, by forcing concessions from the crown and the Barons, during the course of six centuries. *Magna Charta*, which is called the palladium of English liberty, was dated in 1215, and the people of England were not represented in Parliament till the year 1265. Magna Charta established the rights of the Barons and the clergy against the encroachments of royal prerogative; but the commons or people were hardly noticed in that deed. There was but one clause in their favor, which stipulated that, "no villain or rustic should, by any fine, be bereaved of his carts, plows and instruments of husbandry." As for the rest, they were considered as a part of the property belonging to an estate, and were transferred, as other moveables, at the will of their owners. In the succeeding reign, they were permitted to send Representatives to Parliament; and from that time have been gradually assuming their proper degree of consequence in the British Legislature. In such a nation, every law or statute that defines the powers of the crown, and circumscribes them within determinate limits, must be considered as a barrier to guard popular liberty. Every acquisition of freedom must be established as a *right*, and solemnly recognized by the supreme power of the nation; lest it should be again resumed by the crown under pretence of ancient prerogative. . . .

These statutes are however not esteemed because they are unalterable; for the same power that enacted them, can at any moment repeal them; but they are esteemed, because they are barriers erected by the Representatives of the nation, against a power that exists independent of their own choice.

Rights and Self-Restrictions

But the same reasons for such declaratory constitutions do not exist in America, where the supreme power is *the people in their Representatives*. The *Bills of Rights*, prefixed to several of the constitutions of the United States, if considered as assigning the reasons of our separation from a foreign government, or as solemn declarations of right against the encroachments of a foreign jurisdiction, are perfectly rational, and were doubtless necessary. But if they are considered as barriers against the encroachments of our own Legislatures, or as constitutions unalterable by posterity, I venture to pronounce them nugatory, and to the last degree, absurd.

In our governments, there is no power of legislation, independent of the people; no power that has an interest detached from that of the public; consequently there is no power existing against which it is necessary to guard. While our Legislatures therefore remain elective, and the rulers have the same interest in the laws, as the subjects have, the rights of the people will be perfectly secure without any declaration in their favor.

But this is not the principal point. I undertake to prove that a standing *Bill of Rights* is *absurd*, because no constitutions, in a free government, can be unalterable. The present generation have indeed a right to declare what *they* deem a *privilege*; but they have no right to say what the *next* generation shall deem a privilege. A State is a supreme corporation that never dies. Its powers, when it acts for itself, are at all times, equally extensive; and it has the same right to *repeal* a law this year, as it had to *make* it the last. If therefore our posterity are bound by our constitutions, and can neither amend nor annul them, they are to all intents and purposes our slaves.

A Bill That Cannot Be Enforced

But it will be enquired, have we then no right to say, that trial by jury, the liberty of the press, the habeas corpus writ and other invaluable privileges, shall never be infringed nor destroyed? By no means. We have the same right to say that lands shall descend in a particular mode to the heirs of the deceased proprietor, and that such a mode shall never be altered by future generations, as we have to pass a law that the trial by jury shall never be abridged. The right of Jury-trial, which we deem invaluable, may in future cease to be a privilege; or other modes of trial more satisfactory to the people, may be devised. Such an event is neither in impossible nor improbable. Have we then a right to say that our posterity shall not be judges of their own circumstances? The very attempt to make *perpetual* constitutions, is the assumption of a right to control the opinions of future generations; and to legislate for those over whom we have as little authority as we have over a nation in Asia. . . . There are perhaps many laws and regulations, which from their consonance to the eternal rules of justice, will always be good and conformable to the sense of a nation. But most institutions in society, by reason of an unceasing change of circumstances, either become altogether improper or require amendment; and every nation has at all times, the right of judging of its circumstances and determining on the propriety of changing its laws.

The English writers talk much of the omnipotence of Parliament; and yet they seem to entertain some scruples about their right to change particular parts of their constitution. I question much whether Parliament would not hesitate to change, on any occasion, an article of Magna

Charta. [British politician] Mr. [William] Pitt, a few years ago, attempted to reform the mode of representation in Parliament. Immediately an uproar was raised against the measure, as *unconstitutional*. The representation of the kingdom, when first established, was doubtless equal and wise; but by the increase of some cities and boroughs and the depopulation of others, it has become extremely *unequal*. In some boroughs there is scarcely an elector left to enjoy its privileges. If the nation feels no great inconvenience from this change of circumstances, under the old mode of representation, a reform is unnecessary. But if such a change has produced any national evils of magnitude enough to be felt, the present form of electing the Representatives of the nation, however *constitutional*, and venerable for its antiquity, may at any time be amended, if it should be the sense of Parliament. The *expediency* of the alteration must always be a matter of opinion; but all scruples as to the *right* of making it are totally groundless.

Magna Charta may be considered as a contract between two parties, the King and the Barons, and no contract can be altered but by the consent of both parties. But whenever any article of that deed or contract shall become inconvenient or oppressive, the King, Lords and Commons may either amend or annul it at pleasure.

The same reasoning applies to each of the United States, and to the Federal Republic in general.

The U.S. Constitution Needs a Bill of Rights

Melancton Smith

During the Revolutionary War, Melancton Smith (1744–1798) served as a counterespionage agent for the Americans, locating and prosecuting traitors who were loyal to the British. After the war he became extremely rich as a landowner and extremely popular as a New York politician, and in 1785 he was sent to the Constitutional Congress in Philadelphia, Pennsylvania.

While pro-Constitution Federalists James Madison, Alexander Hamilton, and John Jay attempted to drum up support for their position by writing articles under the alias "Publius," Anti-Federalists Melancton Smith and Richard Henry Lee wrote their articles as the "Federal Farmer." In the following article, Smith makes his case for a bill of rights. After masterfully conceding several obvious points, Smith proceeds to dismantle the Federalist position on the issue. According to Smith, a bill of rights would provide an objective basis on which to resolve disputes between the people and their government. If the government chose not to recognize a person's rights, it would have to do so in explicit violation of existing law. It would not be possible for the government to claim that inalienable rights were never guaranteed.

Smith later changed his mind and decided to support the draft Constitution, weakening his standing among Anti-Federalists but broadening his popular appeal. Although he stood to play a major role in the new democracy (Alexander Hamilton once called him "one of the ablest debaters in the country"), Smith's promising political career was cut short when he died of yellow fever in 1798.

Melancton Smith, letter from the "Federal Farmer," January 20, 1788.

As you read, consider the following questions:
1. According to Smith, what is the primary purpose of a bill of rights?
2. How does Smith answer critics who say that a bill of rights is unnecessary because it enumerates rights that are already implicitly reserved to the people?

Having gone through with the organization of the government, I shall now proceed to examine more particularly those clauses which respect its powers. I shall begin with those articles and stipulations which are necessary for accurately ascertaining the extent of powers, and what is given, and for guarding, limiting, and restraining them in their exercise. We often find, these articles and stipulations placed in bills of rights; but they may as well be incorporated in the body of the constitution, as selected and placed by themselves. The constitution, or whole social compact, is but one instrument, no more or less, than a certain number of articles or stipulations agreed to by the people, whether it consists of articles, sections, chapters, bills of rights, or parts of any other denomination, cannot be material.

Many needless observations, and idle distinctions, in my opinion, have been made respecting a bill of rights. On the one hand, it seems to be considered as a necessary distinct limb of the constitution, and as containing a certain number of very valuable articles, which are applicable to all societies: and, on the other, as useless, especially in a federal government, possessing only enumerated power—nay, dangerous, as individual rights are numerous, and not easy to be enumerated in a bill of rights, and from articles, or stipulations, securing some of them, it may be inferred, that others not mentioned are surrendered. There appears to me to be general indefinite propositions without much meaning—and the man who first advanced those of the latter description, in the present case, signed the federal constitution, which directly contradicts him.

The supreme power is undoubtedly in the people, and it

is a principle well established in my mind, that they reserve all powers not expressly delegated by them to those who govern; this is as true in forming a state as in forming a federal government. There is no possible distinction but this founded merely in the different modes of proceeding which take place in some cases. In forming a state constitution, under which to manage not only the great but the little concerns of a community: the powers to be possessed by the government are often too numerous to be enumerated; the people to adopt the shortest way often give general powers, indeed all powers, to the government, in some general words, and then, by a particular enumeration, take back, or rather say they however reserve certain rights as sacred, and which no laws shall be made to violate: hence the idea that all powers are given which are not reserved: but in forming a federal constitution, which ex vi termine, supposes state governments existing, and which is only to manage a few great national concerns, we often find it easier to enumerate particularly the powers to be delegated to the federal head, than to enumerate particularly the individual rights to be reserved; and the principle will operate in its full force, when we carefully adhere to it. When we particularly enumerate the powers given, we ought either carefully to enumerate the rights reserved, or be totally silent about them; we must either particularly enumerate both, or else suppose the particular enumeration of the powers given adequately draws the line between them and the rights reserved, particularly to enumerate the former and not the latter, I think most advisable: however, as men appear generally to have their doubts about these silent reservations, we might advantageously enumerate the powers given, and then in general words, according to the mode adopted in the 2d art. of the confederation, declare all powers, rights and privileges, are reserved, which are not explicitly and expressly given up.

Implicit vs. Explicit Rights

People, and very wisely too, like to be express and explicit about their essential rights, and not to be forced to claim

them on the precarious and unascertained tenure of inferences and general principles, knowing that in any controversy between them and their rulers, concerning those
rights, disputes may be endless, and nothing certain:—But
admitting, on the general principle, that all rights are reserved of course, which are not expressly surrendered, the
people could with sufficient certainty assert their rights on
all occasions, and establish them with ease, still there are
infinite advantages in particularly enumerating many of the
most essential rights reserved in all cases; and as to the less
important ones, we may declare in general terms, that all
not expressly surrendered are reserved. We do not by declarations change the nature of things, or create new truths,
but we give existence, or at least establish in the minds of
the people truths and principles which they might never
otherwise have thought of, or soon forgot.

If a nation means its systems, religious or political, shall
have duration, it ought to recognize the leading principles
of them in the front page of every family book. What is the
usefulness of a truth in theory, unless it exists constantly in
the minds of the people, and has their assent:—we discern
certain rights, as the freedom of the press, and the trial by
jury, &c. which the people of England and of America of
course believe to be sacred, and essential to their political
happiness, and this belief in them is the result of ideas at
first suggested to them by a few able men, and of subsequent experience; while the people of some other countries
hear these rights mentioned with the utmost indifference;
they think the privilege of existing at the will of a despot
much preferable to them. Why this difference amongst beings every way formed alike? The reason of the difference is
obvious—it is the effect of education, a series of notions
impressed upon the minds of the people by examples, pre-
cepts and declarations.

When the people of England got together, at the time
they formed Magna Charta, they did not consider it sufficient, that they were indisputably entitled to certain natural
and unalienable rights, not depending on silent titles, they,

by a declaratory act, expressly recognized them, and explicitly declared to all the world, that they were entitled to enjoy those rights; they made an instrument in writing, and enumerated those they then thought essential, or in danger, and this wise men saw was not sufficient; and therefore, that the people might not forget these rights, and gradually become prepared for arbitrary government, their discerning and honest leaders caused this instrument to be confirmed near forty times, and to be read twice a year in public places, not that it would lose its validity without such confirmations, but to fix the contents of it in the minds of the people, as they successively come upon the stage.— Men, in some countries do not remain free, merely because they are entitled to natural and unalienable rights; men in all countries are entitled to them, not because their ancestors once got together and enumerated them on paper, but because, by repeated negotiations and declarations, all parties are brought to realize them, and of course to believe them to be sacred. Were it necessary, I might shew the wisdom of our past conduct, as a people in not merely comforting ourselves that we were entitled to freedom, but in constantly keeping in view, in addresses, bills of rights, in news-papers, &c. the particular principles on which our freedom must always depend.

Powers Given and Rights Reserved

It is not merely in this point of view, that I urge the engrafting in the constitution additional declaratory articles. The distinction, in itself just, that all powers not given are reserved, is in effect destroyed by this very constitution, as I shall particularly demonstrate—and even independent of this, the people, by adopting the constitution, give many general undefined powers to congress, in the constitutional exercise of which, the rights in question may be effected. Gentlemen who oppose a federal bill of rights, or further declaratory articles, seem to view the subject in a very narrow imperfect manner. These have for their objects, not only the enumeration of the rights reserved, but principally to explain the general powers delegated in certain material points, and to restrain those who exercise them by fixed known boundaries. Many explanations and restrictions necessary and useful, would be much less so, were the people at large all well and fully acquainted with the principles and affairs of government. There appears to be in the constitution, a studied brevity, and it may also be probable, that several explanatory articles were omitted from a circumstance very common. What we have long and early understood ourselves in the common concerns of the community, we are apt to suppose is understood by others, and need not be expressed; and it is not unnatural or uncommon for the ablest men most frequently to make this mistake.

To make declaratory articles unnecessary in an instrument of government, two circumstances must exist; the rights reserved must be indisputably so, and in their nature defined; the powers delegated to the government, must be precisely defined by the words that convey them, and clearly be of such extent and nature as that, by no reasonable construction, they can be made to invade the rights and prerogatives intended to be left in the people.

The first point urged, is, that all power is reserved not expressly given, that particular enumerated powers only are given, that all others are not given, but reserved, and that it is needless to attempt to restrain congress in the exercise of powers they possess not. This reasoning is logical, but of very little importance in the common affairs of men; but the constitution does not appear to respect it even in any view. To prove this, I might cite several clauses in it. I shall only remark on two or three.

By article I, section 9, "No title of nobility shall be granted by congress" was this clause omitted, what power would congress have to make titles of nobility? in what part of the constitution would they find it? The answer must be, that congress would have no such power—that the people, by adopting the constitution, will not part with it. Why then by a negative clause, restrain congress from doing what it would have no power to do? This clause, then, must have no meaning, or imply, that were it omitted, congress would have the power in question, either upon the principle that some general words in the constitution may be so construed as to give it, or on the principle that congress possess the powers not expressly reserved. But this clause was in the confederation, and is said to be introduced into the constitution from very great caution. Even a cautionary provision implies a doubt, at least, that it is necessary; and if so in this case, clearly it is also alike necessary in all similar ones. The fact appears to be, that the people in forming the confederation, and the convention, in this instance, acted, naturally, they did not leave the point to be settled by general principles and logical inferences; but they settle the point in a few words, and all who read them at once understand them.

Clarifying the Rights of the Accused

The trial by jury in criminal as well as in civil causes, has long been considered as one of our fundamental rights, and has been repeatedly recognized and confirmed by most of the state conventions. But the constitution expressly establishes this trial in criminal, and wholly omits it in civil causes. The jury trial in criminal causes, and the benefit of the writ of habeas corpus, are already as effectually established as any of the fundamental or essential rights of the people in the United States. This being the case, why in adopting a federal constitution do we now establish these, and omit all others, or all others, at least with a few exceptions, such as again agreeing there shall be no ex post facto laws, no titles of nobility, &c. We must consider this constitution, when adopted, as the supreme act of the people, and in construing it hereafter, we and our posterity must strictly adhere to the letter and spirit of it, and in no instance depart from them: in construing the federal constitution, it will be not only impracticable, but improper to refer to the state constitutions. They are entirely distinct instruments and inferior acts: besides, by the people's now establishing certain fundamental rights, it is strongly implied, that they are of opinion, that they would not otherwise be secured as a part of the federal system, or be regarded in the federal administration as fundamental.

Further, these same rights, being established by the state constitutions, and secured to the people, our recognizing them now, implies, that the people thought them insecure by the state establishments, and extinguished or put afloat by the new arrangement of the social system, unless re-established.—Further, the people, thus establishing some few rights, and remaining totally silent about others similarly circumstanced, the implication indubitably is, that they mean to relinquish the latter, or at least feel indifferent about them. Rights, therefore, inferred from general principles of reason, being precarious and hardly ascertainable in the common affairs of society, and the people, in forming a federal constitution, explicitly shewing they conceive these rights to be thus circumstanced, and accordingly proceed to enumerate and establish some of them, the conclusion will be, that they have established all which they esteem valuable and sacred. On every principle, then, the people especially having began, ought to go through enumerating, and establish particularly all the rights of individuals, which can by any possibility come in question in making and executing federal laws. I have already observed upon the excellency and importance of the jury trial in civil as well as in criminal causes, instead of establishing it in criminal causes only; we ought to establish it generally;—instead of the clause of forty or fifty words relative to this subject, why not use the language that has always been used in this country, and say, "the people of the United States shall always be entitled to the trial by jury." This would shew the people still hold the fight sacred, and enjoin it upon congress substantially to preserve the jury trial in all cases, according to the usage and custom of the country. I have observed before, that it is the jury trial we want; the little different appendages and modifications tacked to it in the different states, are no more than a drop in the ocean: the jury trial is a solid uniform feature in a free government; it is the substance we would save, not the little articles of form.

These Are Rights and Benefits Individuals Acquire by Compact

Security against ex post facto laws, the trial by jury, and the benefits of the writ of habeas corpus, are but a part of those inestimable rights the people of the United States are entitled to, even in judicial proceedings, by the course of the common law. These may be secured in general words, as in New-York, the Western Territory, &c. by declaring the people of the United States shall always be entitled to judicial proceedings according to the course of the common law, as used and established in the said states.

Perhaps it would be better to enumerate the particular essential rights the people are entitled to in these proceedings, as has been done in many of the states, and as has been done in England. In this case, the people may proceed to declare, that no man shall be held to answer to any offence, till the same be fully described to him; nor to furnish evidence against himself: that, except in the government of the army and navy, no person shall be tried for any offence, whereby he may incur loss of life, or an infamous punishment, until he be first indicted by a grand jury: that every person shall have a right to produce all proofs that may be favourable to him, and to meet the witnesses against him face to face: that every person shall be entitled to obtain right and justice freely and without delay; that all persons shall have a right to be secure from all unreasonable searches and seizures of their persons, houses, papers, or possessions; and that all warrants shall be deemed contrary to this right, if the foundation of them be not previously supported by oath, and there be not in them a special designation of persons or objects of search, arrest, or seizure: and that no person shall be exiled or molested in his person or effects, otherwise than by the judgment of his peers, or according to the law of the land. A celebrated writer observes upon this last article, that in itself it may be said to comprehend the whole end of political society.

These rights are not necessarily reserved, they are established, or enjoyed but in few countries: they are stipulated rights, almost peculiar to British and American laws. In the execution of those laws, individuals, by long custom, by Magna Charta, bills of rights &c. have become entitled to them. A man, at first, by act of parliament, became entitled to the benefits of the writ of habeas corpus—men are entitled to these rights and benefits in the judicial proceedings of our state courts generally: but it will by no means follow, that they will be entitled to them in the federal courts, and have a right to assert them, unless secured and established by the constitution or federal laws. We certainly, in federal processes, might as well claim the benefits of the writ of habeas corpus, as to claim trial by a jury—the right to have council—to have witnesses face to face—to be secure against unreasonable search warrants, &c. was the constitution silent as to the whole of them:—but the establishment of the former, will evince that we could not claim them without it; and the omission of the latter, implies they are relinquished, or deemed of no importance. These are rights and benefits individuals acquire by compact; they must claim them under compacts, or immemorial usage—it is doubtful, at least, whether they can be claimed under immemorial usage in this country; and it is, therefore, we generally claim them under compacts, as charters and constitutions.

The Destruction of Implicit Rights

The people by adopting the federal constitution, give congress general powers to institute a distinct and new judiciary, new courts, and to regulate all proceedings in them; and the further one, that the benefits of the habeas corpus act shall be enjoyed by individuals. Thus general powers being given to institute courts, and regulate their proceedings, with no provision for securing the rights principally in question, may not congress so exercise those powers, and constitutionally too, as to destroy those rights? clearly, in my opinion, they are not in any degree secured. But, admitting the case is only doubtful, would it not be prudent and wise to secure them and remove all doubts, since all agree the people ought to enjoy these valuable rights, a very few men excepted, who seem to be rather of opinion that there is little or nothing in them? Were it necessary I might add many observations to shew their value and political importance.

The constitution will give congress general powers to raise and support armies. General powers carry with them incidental ones, and the means necessary to the end. In the exercise of these powers, is there any provision in the constitution to prevent the quartering of soldiers on the inhabitants? you will answer, there is not. This may sometimes be deemed a necessary measure in the support of armies; on what principle can the people claim the right to be exempt from this burden? they will urge, perhaps, the practice of the country, and the provisions made in some of the state constitutions—they will be answered, that their claim thus to be exempt is not founded in nature, but only in custom and opinion, or at best, in stipulations in some of the state constitutions, which are local, and inferior in their operation, and can have no control over the general government—that they had adopted a federal constitution—had noticed several rights, but had been totally silent about this exemption—that they had given general powers relative to the subject, which, in their operation, regularly destroyed the claim. Though it is not to be presumed, that we are in any immediate danger from this quarter, yet it is fit and proper to establish, beyond dispute, those rights which are particularly valuable to individuals, and essential to the permanency and duration of free government.

An excellent writer observes, that the English, always in possession of their freedom, are frequently unmindful of the value of it: we, at this period, do not seem to be so well off, having, in some instances abused ours; many of us are quite disposed to barter it away for what we call energy, coercion, and some other terms we use as vaguely as that of liberty—There is often as great a rage for change and novelty in politics, as in amusements and fashions.

The Fundamental Right to a Free Press

All parties apparently agree, that the freedom of the press is a fundamental right, and ought not to be restrained by any taxes, duties, or in any manner whatever. Why should not the people, in adopting a federal constitution, declare this, even if there are only doubts about it. But, say the advocates, all powers not given are reserved:—true; but the great question is, are not powers given, in the exercise of which this right may be destroyed? The people's or the printer's claim to a free press, is founded on the fundamental laws, that is, compacts, and state constitutions, made by the people. The people, who can annihilate or alter those constitutions, can annihilate or limit this right. This may be done by giving general powers, as well as by using particular words. No right claimed under a state constitution, will avail against a law of the union, made in pursuance of the federal constitution: therefore the question is, what laws will congress have a right to make by the constitution of the union, and particularly touching the press? By art. 1. sect. 8. congress will have power to lay and collect taxes, duties, imposts and excise. By this congress will clearly have power to lay and collect all kind of taxes whatever—taxes on houses, lands, polls, industry, merchandize, &c.—taxes on deeds, bonds, and all written instruments—on writs, pleas, and all judicial proceedings, on licences, naval officers papers, &c. on newspapers, advertisements, &c. and to require bonds of the naval officers, clerks, printers, &c. to account for the taxes that may become due on papers that go through their hands. Printing, like all other business, must cease when taxed beyond its profits; and it appears to me, that a power to tax the press at discretion, is a power to destroy or restrain the freedom of it. There may be other powers given, in the exercise of which this freedom may be effected; and certainly it is of too much importance to be left thus liable to be taxed, and constantly to constructions and inferences.

A free press is the channel of communication as to mercantile and public affairs; by means of it the people in large countries ascertain each other's sentiments; are enabled to unite, and become formidable to those rulers who adopt improper measures. Newspapers may sometimes be the vehicles of abuse, and of many things not true; but these are but small inconveniencies, in my mind, among many advantages.

A celebrated writer, I have several times quoted, speaking in high terms of the English liberties, says, "lastly the key stone was put to the arch, by the final establishment of the freedom of the press." I shall not dwell longer upon the fundamental rights, to some of which I have attended in this letter, for the same reasons that these I have mentioned, ought to be expressly secured, lest in the exercise of general powers given they may be invaded: it is pretty clear, that some other of less importance, or less in danger, might with propriety also be secured.

The U.S. Constitution Does Not Need a Bill of Rights

Alexander Hamilton

Renowned Revolutionary War hero Alexander Hamilton (1755–1804) worked as a lawyer in New York before being elected to the national Congress. Best known as a vocal advocate for a stronger national government, he was instrumental in establishing the Constitutional Convention in 1787.

In an effort to drum up support, Hamilton, James Madison, and John Jay wrote letters to New York newspapers under the alias "Publius." These letters were published in book form in 1788 as *The Federalist* and are known today as *The Federalist Papers*. Although Madison was the best known of the three, Hamilton was the most prolific contributor, writing more than half of the articles on his own. In this excerpt from an editorial by "Publius," Hamilton responds to critics who feel that the Constitution should be rejected on the grounds that it lacks a bill of rights. Hamilton argues that the Constitution is essentially a bill of rights itself. He contends that specifying particular rights may actually become dangerous by encouraging future leaders to assume that unspecified rights may be freely restricted.

Hamilton did not oppose the Bill of Rights when James Madison brought it up again in 1789 (because his major concern was addressed by the Ninth Amendment, which reserves all unstated rights to the states and the people). Hamilton went on to serve as treasury secretary under George Washington. In 1804, he was killed in a duel by Vice President Aaron Burr.

Publius (Alexander Hamilton), "Federalist No. 84: Certain General and Miscellaneous Objections to the Constitution Considered and Answered," *The Federalist*. New York: McLean's, 1788.

As you read, consider the following questions:
1. According to Hamilton, under what circumstances might a bill of rights be useful?
2. How does Hamilton answer critics who argue that the U.S. Constitution does not adequately protect freedom of the press?

In the course of the foregoing review of the Constitution, I have taken notice of, and endeavored to answer most of the objections which have appeared against it. There, however, remain a few which either did not fall naturally under any particular head or were forgotten in their proper places. . . .

The most considerable of the remaining objections is that the plan of the convention contains no bill of rights. Among other answers given to this, it has been upon different occasions remarked that the constitutions of several of the States are in a similar predicament. I add that New York is of the number. And yet the opposers of the new system, in this State, who profess an unlimited admiration for its constitution, are among the most intemperate partisans of a bill of rights. To justify their zeal in this matter, they allege . . . that the Constitution adopts, in their full extent, the common and statute law of Great Britain, by which many other rights, not expressed in it, are equally secured. . . .

To . . . the pretended establishment of the common and statute law by the Constitution, I answer, that they are expressly made subject "to such alterations and provisions as the legislature shall from time to time make concerning the same." They are therefore at any moment liable to repeal by the ordinary legislative power, and of course have no constitutional sanction. The only use of the declaration was to recognize the ancient law and to remove doubts which might have been occasioned by the Revolution. This consequently can be considered as no part of a declaration of rights, which under our constitutions must be intended as limitations of the power of the government itself.

It has been several times truly remarked that bills of

rights are, in their origin, stipulations between kings and their subjects, abridgements of prerogative in favor of privilege, reservations of rights not surrendered to the prince. Such was MAGNA CHARTA, obtained by the barons, sword in hand, from King John. Such were the subsequent confirmations of that charter by succeeding princes. Such was the PETITION OF RIGHT assented to by Charles I., in the beginning of his reign.

Such, also, was the Declaration of Right presented by the Lords and Commons to the Prince of Orange in 1688, and afterwards thrown into the form of an act of parliament called the Bill of Rights.

It is evident, therefore, that, according to their primitive signification, they have no application to constitutions professedly founded upon the power of the people, and executed by their immediate rep-

Alexander Hamilton

resentatives and servants. Here, in strictness, the people surrender nothing; and as they retain every thing they have no need of particular reservations. "WE, THE PEOPLE of the United States, to secure the blessings of liberty to ourselves and our posterity, do ORDAIN and ESTABLISH this Constitution for the United States of America." Here is a better recognition of popular rights, than volumes of those aphorisms which make the principal figure in several of our State bills of rights, and which would sound much better in a treatise of ethics than in a constitution of government.

But a minute detail of particular rights is certainly far less applicable to a Constitution like that under consideration, which is merely intended to regulate the general political interests of the nation, than to a constitution which has the regulation of every species of personal and private concerns. If, therefore, the loud clamors against the plan of the convention, on this score, are well founded, no epithets of reprobation will be too strong for the constitution of this State. But the truth is, that both of them contain all which, in relation to their objects, is reasonably to be desired.

I go further, and affirm that bills of rights, in the sense and to the extent in which they are contended for, are not only unnecessary in the proposed Constitution, but would even be dangerous.

They would contain various exceptions to powers not granted; and, on this very account, would afford a colorable pretext to claim more than were granted. For why declare that things shall not be done which there is no power to do? Why, for instance, should it be said that the liberty of the press shall not be restrained, when no power is given by which restrictions may be imposed? I will not contend that such a provision would confer a regulating power; but it is evident that it would furnish, to men disposed to usurp, a plausible pretense for claiming that power.

They might urge with a semblance of reason, that the Constitution ought not to be charged with the absurdity of providing against the abuse of an authority which was not given, and that the provision against restraining the liberty of the press afforded a clear implication, that a power to prescribe proper regulations concerning it was intended to be vested in the national government. This may serve as a specimen of the numerous handles which would be given to the doctrine of constructive powers, by the indulgence of an injudicious zeal for bills of rights.

On the subject of the liberty of the press, as much as has been said, I cannot forbear adding a remark or two: in the first place, I observe, that there is not a syllable concerning it in the constitution of this State; in the next, I contend, that whatever has been said about it in that of any other State, amounts to nothing. What signifies a declaration, that "the liberty of the press shall be inviolably preserved"? What is the liberty of the press? Who can give it any definition which would not leave the utmost latitude for evasion? I hold it to be impracticable; and from this I infer, that its security, whatever fine declarations may be inserted in any constitution respecting it, must altogether depend on public opinion, and on the general spirit of the people and of the government. And here, after all, as is intimated upon another occasion, must we seek for the only solid basis of all our rights.

The Constitution Is a Bill of Rights

There remains but one other view of this matter to conclude the point. The truth is, after all the declamations we have heard, that the Constitution is itself, in every rational sense, and to every useful purpose, A BILL OF RIGHTS. The several bills of rights in Great Britain form its Constitution, and conversely the constitution of each State is its bill of rights. And the proposed Constitution, if adopted, will be the bill of rights of the Union. Is it one object of a bill of rights to declare and specify the political privileges of the citizens in the structure and administration of the government? This is done in the most ample and precise manner in the plan of the convention; comprehending various precautions for the public security, which are not to be found in any of the State constitutions. Is another object of a bill of rights to define certain immunities and modes of proceeding, which are relative to personal and private concerns? This we have seen has also been attended to, in a variety of cases, in the same plan. Adverting therefore to the substantial meaning of a bill of rights, it is absurd to allege that it is not to be found in the work of the convention. It may be said that it does not go far enough, though it will not be easy to make this appear; but it can with no propriety be contended that there is no such thing. It certainly must be immaterial what mode is observed as to the order of declaring the rights of the citizens, if they are to be found in any part of the instrument which establishes the government. And hence it must be apparent, that much of what has been said on this subject rests merely on verbal and nominal distinctions, entirely foreign from the substance of the thing.

The Bill of Rights Proposal

James Madison

James Madison (1750–1836) was an aggressive critic of religious persecution in his home state of Virginia. For the first ten years of his political career, he served in both Virginia's local legislature and the national Congress; by 1787, he had become an experienced lawmaker. Virginia sent Madison to the Constitutional Convention, where his role was so prominent and decisive that he is now remembered as the "Father of the Constitution."

Madison initially felt that a bill of rights was unnecessary, but he agreed to propose one in 1789. In the following speech to Congress, Madison outlines his reasons for doing so. He believed that the strongest argument in favor of a bill of rights was that it would relieve public fears of governmental abuses.

In 1809 James Madison became the fourth president of the United States.

As you read, consider the following questions:
1. What is Madison's primary motive in proposing a bill of rights?
2. Why is it more necessary to guard against abuse of power in the legislative than the executive branch, according to Madison?
3. How does Madison answer critics who argue that rights not listed in a bill of rights would be assigned to the government and not reserved to the people?

James Madison, "Amendments to the Constitution," 1789.

I will state my reasons why I think it proper to propose amendments; and state the amendments themselves, so far as I think they ought to be proposed. If I thought I could fulfil the duty which I owe to myself and my constituents, to let the subject pass over in silence, I most certainly should not trespass upon the indulgence of this house. But I cannot do this; and am therefore compelled to beg a patient hearing to what I have to lay before you. And I do most sincerely believe that if congress will devote but one day to this subjects, so far as to satisfy the public that we do not disregard their wishes, it will have a salutary influence on the public councils, and prepare the way for a favorable reception of our future measures.

It appears to me that this house is bound by every motive of prudence, not to let the first session pass over without proposing to the state legislatures some things to be incorporated into the constitution, as will render it as acceptable to the whole people of the United States, as it has been found acceptable to a majority of them. I wish, among other reasons why something should be done, that those who have been friendly to the adoption of this constitution, may have the opportunity of proving to those who were opposed to it, that they were as sincerely devoted to liberty and a republican government, as those who charged them with wishing the adoption of this constitution in order to lay the foundation of an aristocracy or despotism. It will be a desirable thing to extinguish from the bosom of every member of the community any apprehensions, that there are those among his countrymen who wish to deprive them of the liberty for which they valiantly fought and honorably bled. And if there are amendments desired, of such a nature as will not injure the constitution, and they can be ingrafted so as to give satisfaction to the doubting part of our fellow citizens; the friends of the federal government will evince that spirit of deference and concession for which they have hitherto been distinguished.

It cannot be a secret to the gentlemen in this house, that,

notwithstanding the ratification of this system of government by eleven of the thirteen United States, in some cases unanimously, in others by large majorities; yet still there is a great number of our constituents who are dissatisfied with it; among whom are many respectable for their talents, their patriotism, and respectable for the jealousy they have for their liberty, which, though mistaken in its object, is laudable in its motive. There is a great body of the people falling under this description, who at present feel much inclined to join their support to the cause of federalism, if they were satisfied in this one point: We ought not to disregard their inclination, but, on principles of amity and moderation, conform to their wishes, and expressly declare the great rights of mankind secured under this constitution. The acquiescence which our fellow citizens shew under the government, calls upon us for a like return of moderation. But perhaps there is a stronger motive than this for our going into a consideration of the subject; it is to provide those securities for liberty which are required by a part of the community. I allude in a particular manner to those two states [North Carolina and Rhode Island] who have not thought fit to throw themselves into the bosom of the confederacy: it is a desirable thing, on our part as well as theirs, that a re-union should take place as soon as possible. . . .

But I will candidly acknowledge, that, over and above all these considerations, I do conceive that the constitution may be amended; that is to say, if all power is subject to abuse, that then it is possible the abuse of the powers of the general government may be guarded against in a more secure manner than is now done, while no one advantage, arising from the exercise of that power, shall be damaged or endangered by it. We have in this way something to gain, and, if we proceed with caution, nothing to lose; and in this case it is necessary to proceed with caution; for while we feel all these inducements to go into a revisal of the constitution, we must feel for the constitution itself, and make that revisal a moderate one. I should be unwilling to see a door opened for a re-consideration of the whole structure of the government, for a re-consideration of the principles and the substance of the powers given; because I doubt, if such a door was opened, if we should be very likely to stop at that point which would be safe to the government itself: But I do wish to see a door opened to consider, so far as to incorporate those provisions for the security of rights, against which I believe no serious objection has been made by any class of our constituents, such as would be likely to meet with the concurrence of two-thirds of both houses, and the approbation of three-fourths of the state legislatures. I will not propose a single alteration which I do not wish to see take place, as intrinsically proper in itself, or proper because it is wished for by a respectable number of my fellow citizens; and therefore I shall not propose a single alteration but is likely to meet the concurrence required by the constitution.

An Objection That Can Be Resolved

There have been objections of various kinds made against the constitution: Some were levelled gainst its structure, because the president was without a council; because the senate, which is a legislative body, had judicial powers in trials on impeachments; and because the powers of that body were compounded in other respects, in a manner that did not correspond with a particular theory; because it grants more power than is supposed to be necessary for every good purpose; and controuls the ordinary powers of the state governments. I know some respectable characters who opposed this government on these grounds; but I believe that the great mass of the people who opposed it, disliked it because it did not contain effectual provison against encroachments on particular rights, and those safeguards which they have been long accustomed to have interposed between them and the magistrate who exercised the sovereign power: nor ought we to consider them safe, while a great number of our fellow citizens think these securities necessary.

It has been a fortunate thing that the objection to the government has been made on the ground I stated; because it will be practicable on that ground to obviate the objection, so far as to satisfy the public mind that their liberties will be perpetual, and this without endangering any part of the constitution, which is considered as essential to the existence of the government by those who promoted its adoption. . . .

I will own that I never considered this provision [for a bill of rights] so essential to the federal constitution, as to make it improper to ratify it, until such an amendment was added; at the same time, I always conceived, that in a certain form and to a certain extent, such a provision was neither improper nor altogether useless. I am aware, that a great number of the most respectable friends to the government and champions for republican liberty, have thought such a provision, not only unnecessary, but even improper, nay, I believe some have gone so far as to think it even dangerous. Some policy has been made use of perhaps by gentlemen on both sides of the question: I acknowledge the ingenuity of those arguments which were drawn against the constitution, by a comparison with the policy of Great-Britain, in establishing a declaration of rights; but there is too great a difference in the case to warrant the comparison: therefore the arguments drawn from that source, were in a great measure inapplicable. In the declaration of rights which that country has established, the truth is, they have gone no farther, than to raise a barrier against the power of the crown; the power of the legislature is left altogether indefinite. . . . The freedom of the press and rights of conscience, those choicest privileges of the people, are unguarded in the British constitution. . . .

Limiting the Power of Government

The people of many states, have thought it necessary to raise barriers against power in all forms and departments of government, and I am inclined to believe, if once bills of rights are established in all the states as well as the federal constitution, we shall find that altho' some of them are rather unimportant, yet, upon the whole, they will have a salutary tendency.

It may be said, in some instances they do no more than state the perfect equality of mankind; this to be sure is an absolute truth, yet it is not absolutely necessary to be inserted at the head of a constitution.

In some instances they assert those rights which are exercised by the people in forming and establishing a plan of government. In other instances, they specify those rights which are retained when particular powers are given up to be exercised by the legislature. In other instances, they specify positive rights, which may seem to result from the nature of the compact. Trial by jury cannot be considered as a natural right, but a right resulting from the social compact which regulates the action of the community, but is as essential to secure the liberty of the people as any one of the pre-existent rights of nature. In other instances they lay down dogmatic maxims with respect to the construction of the government; declaring, that the legislative, executive, and judicial branches shall be kept separate and distinct: Perhaps the best way of securing this in practice is to provide such checks, as will prevent the encroachment of the one upon the other.

But whatever may be [the] form which the several states have adopted in making declarations in favor of particular rights, the great object in view is to limit and qualify the powers of government, by excepting out of the grant of power those cases in which the government ought not to act, or to act only in a particular mode. They point these exceptions sometimes against the abuse of the executive power, sometimes against the legislative, and, in some cases, against the community itself; or, in other words, against the majority in favor of the minority.

"By the Majority Against the Minority"

In our government it is, perhaps, less necessary to guard against the abuse in the executive department than any other; because it is not the stronger branch of the system, but the weaker: It therefore must be levelled against the legislative, for it is the most powerful, and most likely to be abused, because it is under the least controul; hence, so far as a declaration of rights can tend to prevent the exercise of undue power, it cannot be doubted but such declaration is proper. But I confess that I do conceive, that in a government modified like this of the United States, the great danger lies rather in the abuse of the community than in the legislative body. The prescriptions in favor of liberty, ought to be levelled against that quarter where the greatest danger lies, namely, that which possesses the highest prerogative of power: But this [is] not found in either the executive or legislative departments of government, but in the body of the people, operating by the majority against the minority.

It may be thought all paper barriers against the power of the community are too weak to be worthy of attention. I am sensible they are not so strong as to satisfy gentlemen of every description who have seen and examined thoroughly the texture of such a defence; yet, as they have a tendency to impress some degree of respect for them, to establish the public opinion in their favor, and rouse the attention of the whole community, it may be one mean to controul the majority from those acts to which they might be otherwise inclined.

It has been said by way of objection to a bill of rights, by many respectable gentlemen out of doors, and I find opposition on the same principles likely to be made by gentlemen on this floor, that they are unnecessary articles of a republican government, upon the presumption that the people have those rights in their own hands, and that is the proper place for them to rest. It would be a sufficient answer to say that this objection lies against such provisons under the state governments as well as under the general government; and there are, I believe, but few gentlemen who are inclined to push their theory so far as to say that a declaration of rights in those cases is either ineffectual or improper.

Answering Critics

It has been said that in the federal government they are unnecessary, because the powers are enumerated, and it follows that all that are not granted by the constitution are retained: that the constitution is a bill of powers, the great residuum being the rights of the people; and therefore a bill of rights cannot be so necessary as if the residuum was thrown into the hands of the government. I admit that these arguments are not entirely without foundation; but they are not conclusive to the extent which has been supposed. It is true the powers of the general government are circumscribed; they are directed to particular objects; but even if government keeps within those limits, it has certain discretionary powers with respect to the means, which may admit of abuse to a certain extent . . . the direction of the legislature: may not general warrants be considered necessary for this purpose, as well as for some purposes which it was supposed at the framing of their constitutions the state governments had in view. If there was reason for restraining the state governments from exercising this power, there is like reason for restraining the federal government.

It may be said, because it has been said, that a bill of rights is not necessary, because the establishment of this government has not repealed those declarations of rights which are added to the several state constitutions: that those rights of the people, which had been established by the most solemn act, could not be annihilated by a subsequent act of the people, who meant, and declared at the head of the instrument, that they ordained and established a new system, for the express purpose of securing to themselves and posterity the liberties they had gained by an arduous conflict.

I admit the force of this observation, but I do not look upon it to be conclusive. In the first place, it is too uncertain ground to leave this provision upon, if a provision is at all necessary to secure rights so important as many of those I have mentioned are conceived to be, by the public in general, as well as those in particular who opposed the adoption of this constitution. Beside some states have no bills of rights, there are others provided with very defective ones, and there are others whose bills of rights are not only defective, but absolutely improper; instead of securing some in the full extent which republican principles would require, they limit them too much to agree with the common ideas of liberty.

It has been objected also against a bill of rights, that, by enumerating particular exceptions to the grant of power, it would disparage those rights which were not placed in that enumeration, and it might follow by implication, that those rights which were not singled out, were intended to be assigned into the hands of the general government, and were consequently insecure. This is one of the most plausible arguments I have ever heard urged against the admission of a bill of rights into this system; but, I conceive, that may be guarded against. I have attempted it, as gentlemen may see by turning to the last clause of the 4th resolution [upon which the Ninth Amendment was later based].

"Guardians of Those Rights"

It has been said, that it is necessary to load the constitution with [the Bill of Rights] because it was not found effectual in the constitution of the particular states. It is true, there are a few particular states in which some of the most valuable articles have not, at one time or other, been violated; but does it not follow but they may have, to a certain degree, a salutary effect against the abuse of power. If they are incorporated into the constitution, independent tribunals of justice will consider themselves in a peculiar manner the guardians of those rights; they will be an impenetrable bulwark against every assumption of power in the legislative or executive; they will be naturally led to resist every encroachment upon rights expressly stipulated for in the constitution by the declaration of rights. Beside this security, there is a great probability that such a declaration in the federal system would be enforced; because the state legislatures will jealously and closely watch the operation of this government, and be able to resist with more effect every assumption of power than any other power on earth can do; and the greatest opponents to a federal government admit the state legislatures to be sure guardians of the people's liberty. I conclude from this view of the subject, that it will be proper in itself, and highly politic, for the tranquility of the public mind, and the stability of the government, that we should offer something, in the form I have proposed, to be incorporated in the system of government, as a declaration of the rights of the people. . . .

Fortifying the Rights of the People

These are the points on which I wish to see a revision of the constitution take place. How far they will accord with the sense of this body, I cannot take upon me absolutely to determine; but I believe every gentleman will readily admit that nothing is in contemplation, so far as I have mentioned, that can endanger the beauty of the government in any one important feature, even in the eyes of its most sanguine admirers. I have proposed nothing that does not appear to me as proper in itself, or eligible as patronised by a respectable number of our fellow citizens; and if we can make the constitution better in the opinion of those who are opposed to it, without weakening its frame, or abridging its usefulness, in the judgment of those who are attached to it, we act the part of wise and liberal men to make such alterations as shall produce that effect.

Having done what I conceived was my duty, in bringing before this house the subject of amendments, and also stated such as wish for and approve, and offered the reasons which occurred to me in their support; I shall content myself for the present with moving, that a committee be appointed to consider of and report such amendments as ought to be proposed by congress to the legislatures of the states, to become, if ratified by three-fourths thereof, part of the constitution of the United States. By agreeing to this motion, the subject may be going on in the committee, while other important business is proceeding to a conclusion in the house. I should advocate greater dispatch in the business of amendments, if I was not convinced of the absolute necessity there is of pursuing the organization of the government; because I think we should obtain the confidence of our fellow citizens, in proportion as we fortify the rights of the people against the encroachments of the government.

2

FREEDOM OF EXPRESSION

CHAPTER PREFACE

Congress shall make no law . . . abridging the freedom of speech, or of the press, or the right of the people peaceably to assemble, and to petition the government for a redress of grievances.

—Amendment I

Sometimes described as the "first freedom," the right to free expression is generally regarded as one of the most important individual rights guaranteed by the Constitution and as essential to any viable democracy. "Our liberty depends on the freedom of the press," Thomas Jefferson once wrote, "and that cannot be limited without being lost."

Yet the individual right to free expression cannot be interpreted as completely absolute, because there are obvious cases where speech itself can cause as much direct damage as physical violence. If someone shouts "Fire!" in a crowded building, lies in the process of committing fraud, or shares top secret public safety data with terrorist organizations, federal and state governments have the power to punish that behavior. Both sides of the free speech debate agree that there is an individual right to free expression and that some public interests must be protected by law. Most free speech controversies can be described as legitimate disagreements over how those two needs can be met.

During World War I the U.S. government restricted speech advocating violent revolution by passing the Sedition Act of 1918. The reasoning at the time was that this speech could bring about violent social movements that could present a very real danger to the United States and its people, and the Supreme Court affirmed this line of reasoning by declaring the legislation to be constitutional in *U.S. v. Abrams* (1919). Yet antigovernment speech was probably exactly the sort of speech that the nation's founders intended to protect; after all, they were revolutionaries themselves. Over time, the Court took a more libertarian view toward antigovernment speech and, in a series of later rulings, made it impossible for Congress to enforce laws restricting sedition.

There have also been attempts over the years to restrict hate speech. Although abusive language can already be prohibited if it is disruptive or clearly intended to provoke a violent reaction, the Court has historically determined that the First Amendment protects all ideas from content-based restriction. In other words, racist speech can be restricted if it violates other laws but cannot be restricted solely on the grounds that it is racist. In *Skokie v. Illinois* (1977), the Court ruled that a small town heavily populated with Holocaust survivors could not pass a law preventing neo-Nazis from marching in their streets. The Court has also traditionally found that cross burning, a form of racist intimidation historically practiced by the Ku Klux Klan, is a form of protected expression (although it ruled in *Black v. Virginia* (2003) that cross burning can be restricted in cases where it could reasonably be interpreted as a personal threat).

In most cases, both advocates and opponents of speech and press restriction believe that they are protecting American citizens. The readings in this chapter represent the perspectives of those who, in the course of American history, have taken what they considered to be a moral and humane stand on issues related to the freedom of expression guaranteed by the First Amendment.

Criticism of the Government Should Be Permitted

James Burgh

The First Amendment to the U.S. Constitution protects the right to free expression, including expression of political opinions. Many who voted for the amendment were personally familiar with the British "seditious libel" laws, which criminalized personal criticism of public officials. In the following excerpt from a book published in 1775, Scottish philosopher James Burgh (1714–1775) maintains that such laws are unjust. Advocates of the First Amendment sought to prevent similar laws from being passed in the United States.

Burgh was a close friend of Benjamin Franklin and a considerable influence on Thomas Jefferson. A voracious reader who loved philosophical debates, Burgh decided to put some of his ideas down on paper in *The Dignity of Human Nature* (1754). Most of his later writings dealt with political reforms, focusing on free speech and the right to dissent (once writing that "if you punish the slanderer, you deter the fair inquirer"). This excerpt is from his last book, the three-volume *Political Disquisitions*.

As you read, consider the following questions:
1. According to Lord Chesterfield (as quoted by Burgh), how can public figures best protect their reputation?
2. Why does Burgh disagree with laws that criminalize libel?

In an inquiry into public abuses no one will wonder to find punishment inflicted by government upon complainers,

James Burgh, *Political Disquisitions*. 3 vols. London: Robert Bell and William Woodhouse, 1774–1775.

reckoned as an abuse; for it certainly is one of the most atrocious abuses, that a free subject should be restrained in his inquiries into the conduct of those who undertake to manage his affairs; I mean the administrators of government: for all such are undertakers, and are answerable for what they undertake: but if it be dangerous and penal to inquire into their conduct, the state may be ruined by their blunders, or by their villanies, beyond the possibility of redress.

There seems to be somewhat unnatural in attempting to lay a restraint on those who would criticise the conduct of men who undertake to do other people's business. It is an offence, if we remark on the decision of a court of law, on the proceedings of either house of parliament, or of the administration; all whose proceedings we are immediately concerned in. At the same time, if a man builds a house for himself, marries a wife for himself, or writes a book, by which the public gets more than the author, it is no offence to make very severe and unjust remarks.

Are Judges, Juries, Counsellors, Members of the House of Commons, Peers, Secretaries of State, or Kings, infallible? Or are they short-sighted, and perhaps interested, mortals?

Speech Against Political Leaders

In a petition to parliament, a bill in chancery, and proceedings at law, libellous words are not punishable; because freedom of speech and writing are indispensably necessary to the carrying on of business. But it may be said, there is no necessity for a private writer to be indulged the liberty of attacking the conduct of those who take upon themselves to govern the state. The answer is easy, viz. That all history shews the necessity, in order to the preservation of liberty, of every subject's having a watchful eye on the conduct of Kings, Ministers, and Parliament, and of every subject's being not only secured, but encouraged in alarming his fellow-subjects on occasion of every attempt upon public liberty, and that private, independent subjects *only* are likely to give fair warning of such attempts; their betters (as to rank and fortune) being more likely to conceal, than detect the abuses committed by those in power. If, therefore, private writers are to be intimidated in shewing their fidelity to their country, the principal security of liberty is taken away.

Punishing libels public or private is foolish, because it does not answer the end, and because the end is a bad one, if it could be answered.

The Attorney General De Grey confessed in the House of Commons, A.D. 1770, "that his power of filing informations *ex officio* is an odious power, and that it does not answer the purpose intended; for that he had not been able to bring any libeller to justice." Mr. Pownal shewed that power to be illegal and unconstitutional; for that, according to law, no *Englishman* is to be brought upon his trial, but by presentment of his country; a few particular cases excepted.

When the lawyers say a libel is criminal, though true, they mean, because it is, according to them, a breach of the peace, and tends to excite revenge. They allow, that the *falsehood* of the charge is an aggravation, and that, therefore, the person libelled has no right to damages, if the charges laid against him be *true*. But by this rule it should seem, that the *truth* of the libel should take away all its criminality. For if I have no right to damages, I have no pretence to seek revenge. Therefore to libel me for what I cannot affirm myself to be innocent of, is no breach of the peace, as it does not naturally tend to excite revenge, but rather ingenuous shame and reformation.

Reputation and Politics

Let us hear on this subject the excellent Lord Chesterfield on the bill for licensing the stage, A.D. 1737.

In public, as well as private life, the only way to prevent being ridiculed or censured, is to avoid all ridiculous or wicked measures, and to pursue such only as are virtuous and worthy. The people never endeavor to ridicule those they love and esteem, nor will they suffer them to be ridiculed. If any one attempts it, their ridicule returns upon the author; he makes himself only the object of public hatred and contempt. The actions or behaviour of a private man may pass unobserved, and consequently unapplauded and uncensured; but the actions of these in high stations, can neither pass without notice nor without censure or applause; and therefore an administration without esteem, without authority, among the people, let their power be ever so great or ever so arbitrary, will be ridiculed: the severest edicts, the most terrible punishments cannot prevent it. If any man, therefore, thinks he has been censured, if any man thinks he has been ridiculed, upon any of our public theatres, let him examine his actions he will find the cause, let him alter his conduct he will find a remedy. As no man is perfect, as no man is infallible, the greatest may err, the most circumspect may be guilty of some piece of ridiculous behavior. It is not licentiousness, it is an useful liberty always indulged the stage in a free country, that some great men may there meet with a just reproof, which none of their friends will be free enough, or rather faithful enough to give them. Of this we have a famous influence in the Roman history. The great Pompey, after the many victories he had obtained, and the great conquests he had made, had certainly a good title to the esteem of the people of Rome. Yet that great man by some error in his conduct, became an object of general dislike; and therefore in the representation of an old play, when Diphilus the actor came to repeat these words, *Nostrâ miseriâ tu es magnus*, the audience immediately applied them to Pompey, who at that time was as well known by the name of Magnus as by the name Pompey, and were so highly pleased with the satire, that, as Cicero tells us, they made the actor repeat the words one hundred times over. An account of this was immediately sent to Pompey, who, instead of resenting it as an injury, was so wise as to take it for a just reproof. He examined his conduct, he altered his measures, he regained by degrees the esteem of the people, and then he neither feared the wit, nor felt the satire of the stage. This is an example which ought to be followed by great men in all countries.

Even the cruel Tiberius, when in good humour, could say, In a free state, the mind and the tongue "ought to be free." Titus defied any one to scandalize him. Trajan published absolute liberty of speech and writing. Constantine, when he was told that some ill-disposed persons had battered his head and face, meaning those of his statue, felt himself all about those parts, and told his courtiers, he found nothing amiss; desiring that they would take no trouble about finding out the violators of the statue.

Honesty and Public Life
Mr. Gordon allows the maxim, that a libel is not the less a libel for being true. But this holds, he says, only in respect of *private* characters; and it is quite otherwise, when the crimes of men affect the *public*. We are to take care of the public safety at all adventures. And the loss of an individual's, or a whole ministry's *political* characters, ought to be despised, when put in competition with the fate of a kingdom. Therefore no free subject ought to be under the least restraint in respect to accusing the greatest, so long as his accusation strikes only at the *political* conduct of the accused: his private we have no right to meddle with, but in so far as a known vicious private character indicates an unfitness for public power or truth.

But it may be said, this is a grievous hardship on those who undertake the administration of a nation; that they are to run the hazard of being thus publicly accused of corruption, embezzlement, and other political crimes, without having it in their power to punish their slanderers. To this I answer, It is no hardship at all, but the unavoidable inconvenience attendant upon a high station, which he who dislikes must avoid, and keep himself private. Cato was forty times tried. But we do not think the worse of Cato for this.

If a statesman is liable to be falsely accused, let him comfort himself by recollecting, that he is well paid. An ensign is liable to be killed in war; and he has but 3 *s*. 6 *d*. a day. If a statesman has designedly behaved amiss, he ought to be punished with the utmost severity; because the injury he has done, is unboundedly extensive. If he has injured the public through weakness, and without wicked intention, he is still punishable; because he ought not to have thrust himself into a station for which he was unfit. But, indeed, these cases are so rare (want of *honesty* being the general cause of maladministration), that it is scarce worth while to touch upon them.

If a statesman is falsely accused, he has only to clear his character, and he appears in a fairer light than before. He must not insist on punishing his accuser: for the public security requires, that there be no danger in accusing those who undertake the administration of national affairs. The punishment of political satyrists gains credit to their writings, nor do unjust govenments reap any fruit from such severities, but insults to themselves, and honour to those whom they prosecute.

A libel is in fact (criminally speaking) a *non entity, i.e.* there is no such offence as scandal. For if the punishment was taken away, the whole of the evil would be taken away, because nobody would regard scandal; but people would believe every person's character to be what they knew it.

Unfair Criticism of the Government Should Be Restricted

John Marshall

As the third chief justice of the U.S. Supreme Court, John Marshall (1755–1835) almost single-handedly established the Supreme Court as a full and autonomous branch of the U.S. government. Before his tenure, the Court played an interpretative role and focused on enforcing existing laws. Marshall expanded its role with his ruling in *Marbury v. Madison* (1803), holding the Court responsible for striking down unconstitutional laws and resolving disputes between the federal and state governments.

Before becoming chief justice, Marshall served in the Virginia legislature during a turbulent period. Facing constant criticism and a possible war with France, Federalist president John Adams signed the Alien and Sedition Acts of 1798, which criminalized antigovernment speech. Adams's goal was to silence critics who supported Democratic Republican presidential candidate Thomas Jefferson. The Sedition Act quickly became extremely unpopular. In response to the act, one critic, James Madison, drafted the Virginia Resolutions of 1798, which condemned the Sedition Act as unconstitutional. In this excerpt from a speech he delivered before the Virginia legislature, future chief justice John Marshall defends the act against these charges and concludes that it does not violate the First Amendment.

The Sedition Act was so unpopular with the American people that by the time it expired in 1801, Thomas Jefferson had been elected president by a landslide. No Federalist Party candidate would ever be elected to national office again.

John Marshall, "Report to the Minority on the Virginia Resolutions," January 22, 1799.

As you read, consider the following questions:
1. Why does Marshall consider antigovernment speech dangerous?
2. According to Marshall, how can the Sedition Act be reconciled with the First Amendment?

To contend that there does not exist a power to punish writings coming within the description of this law [The Sedition Act], would be to assert the inability of our nation to preserve its own peace, and to protect themselves from the attempts of wicked citizens, who, incapable of quiet themselves, are incessantly employed in devising means to disturb the public repose.

Government is instituted and preserved for the general happiness and safety—the people therefore are interested in its preservation, and have a right to adopt measures for its security, as well against secret plots as open hostility. But government cannot be thus secured, if by falsehood and malicious slander, it is to be deprived of the confidence and affection of the people. It is vain to urge that truth will prevail, and that slander, when detected, recoils on the calumniator. The experience of the world, and our own experience, prove that a continued course of defamation will at length sully the fairest reputation, and will throw suspicion on the purest conduct. Although the calumnies of the factious and discontented may not poison the minds of the majority of the citizens, yet they will infect a very considerable number, and prompt them to deeds destructive of the public peace and dangerous to the general safety.

This, the people have a right to prevent: and therefore, in all the nations of the earth, where presses are known, some corrective of their licentiousness has been deemed indispensable. But it is contended that though this may be theoretically true, such is the peculiar structure of our government, that this power has either never been confided to, or has been withdrawn from the legislature of this union.—We will examine these positions. The power of making all laws which shall be necessary and proper for carrying into execution all powers vested by the constitution in the government of the United States, or in any department or officer thereof, is by the concluding clause of the eighth section of the first article, expressly delegated to congress. This clause is admitted to authorize congress to pass any act for the punishment of those who would resist the execution of the laws, because such an act would be incontestably necessary and proper for carrying into execution the powers vested in the government. . . .

To punish all malicious calumnies against an individual with an intent to defame him, is a wrong on the part of the calumniator, and an injury to the individual, for which the laws afford redress. To write or print these calumnies is such an aggravation of the crime, as to constitute an offence against the government, and the author of the libel is subject to the additional punishment which may be inflicted under an indictment. To publish malicious calumnies against government itself, is a wrong on the part of the calumniator, and an injury to all those who have an interest in the government. Those who have this interest and have sustained the injury, have the natural right to an adequate remedy. The people of the United States have a common interest in their govenment, and sustain in common the injury which affects that government. The people of the United States therefore have a right to the remedy for that injury, and are substantially the party seeking redress. By the 2d section of the 3d article of the constitution, the judicial power of the United States is extended to controversies to which the United States shall be a party; and by the same article it is extended to all cases in law and equity arising under the constitution, the laws of the United States, and treaties made or which shall be made under their authority. What are cases arising under the constitution, as contradistinguished from those which arise under the laws made in pursuance thereof? They must be cases triable by a rule which exists independent of any act of the legislature of the union. That rule is the common or unwritten law which pervades all America, and which declaring libels against government to be a punishable offence, applies itself to and protects any government which the will of the people may establish. The judicial power of the United States, then, being extended to the punishment of libels against the government, as a common law offence, arising under the constitution which create the government, the general clause gives to the legislature of the union the right to make such laws as shall give that power effect.

That such was the contemporaneous construction of the constitution, is obvious from one of the amendments which have been made to it. The [first] amendment which declares, that Congress shall make no law abridging the liberty of the press, is a general construction made by all America on the original instrument admitting its application to the subject. It would have been certainly unnecessary thus to have modified the legislative powers of Congress concerning the press, if the power itself does not exist.

But altho' the original constitution may be supposed to have enabled the government to defend itself against false and malicious libels, endangering the peace, and threatening the tranquility of the American people, yet it is contended that the [first] amendment to that instrument, has deprived it of this power.

The amendment is in these words,—"Congress shall make no law respecting an establishment of religion, or prohibiting the free exercise thereof, or ABRIDGING the freedom of speech or of the press."

Sedition and the First Amendment

In a solemn instrument, as is a constitution, words are well weighed and considered before they are adopted. A remarkable diversity of expression is not used, unless it be designed to manifest a difference of intention. Congress is prohibited from making any law RESPECTING a religious establishment, but not from making any law RESPECTING the press. When the power of Congress relative to the press is to be limited, the word RESPECTING is dropt, and

Congress is only restrained from passing any law ABRIDG-ING its liberty. This difference of expression with respect to religion and the press, manifests a difference of intention with respect to the power of the national legislature over those subjects, both in the person who drew, and in those who adopted this amendment.

All ABRIDGMENT of the freedom of the press is forbidden, but it is only an ABRIDGMENT of that freedom which is forbidden. It becomes then necessary in order to determine whether the act in question be unconstitutional or not, to inquire whether it does in fact ABRIDGE the freedom of the press.

The act is believed not to have that operation, for two reasons.

1st. A punishment of the licentiousness is not considered as a restriction of the freedom of the press,

2d. The act complained of does not punish any writing not before punishable, nor does it inflict a more severe penalty than that to which the same writing was before liable.

John Marshall

If by freedom of the press is meant a perfect exemption from all punishment for whatever may be published, that freedom never has, and most probably never will exist. It is known to all, that the person who writes or publishes a libel, may be both sued and indicted, and must bear the penalty which the judgment of his country inflicts upon him. It is also known to all that the person who shall libel the government of the state, is for that offence, punishable in the like manner. Yet this liability to punishment for slanderous and malicious publications has never been considered as detracting from the liberty of the press. In fact the liberty of the press is a term which has a definite and appropriate signification, completely understood. It signifies a liberty to publish, free from previous restraint, any thing and every thing at the discretion of the printer only, but not the liberty of spreading with impunity false and scandalous slanders which may destroy the peace and mangle the reputation of an individual or of a community.

If this definition of the term be correct, and it is presumed that its correctness is not to be questioned, then a law punishing the authors and publishers of false, malicious and scandalous libels can be no attack on the liberty of the press.

Does the First Amendment Prohibit Punishment After the Fact?

But the act complained of is no abridgment of the liberty of the press, for another reason. It does not punish any writing not before punishable, nor does it inflict a heavier penalty than the same writing was before liable to.

No man will deny, that at common law, the author and publisher of a false, scandalous and malicious libel against the government or an individual, were subject to fine and imprisonment, at the discretion of the judge. Nor will it be denied, that previous to our revolution, the common law was the law of the land throughout the now United States.

We believe it to be a principle incontestibly true, that a change of government does not dissolve obligations previously created, does not annihilate existing laws, and dissolve the bonds of society; but that a People passing from one form of government to another, retain in full force all their municipal institutions not necessarily changed by the change of government. If this be true, then the common law continued to be the law of the land after the revolution, and was of complete obligation even before the act of our Assembly for its adoption. Whether similar acts have been passed by the legislature of other states or not, it is certain that in every state the common law is admitted to be in full force, except as it may have been altered by the statute law. The only question is, whether the doctrines of the common law are applicable to libels against the government of the United States, as well as to libels against the governments of particular states. For such a distinction there seems to be no sufficient reason. It is not to a magistrate of this or that description that the rules of the common law apply. That he is a magistrate, that he is cloathed with the authority of the laws, that he is invested with power by the people, is a sufficient title to the protection of the common law. The government of the United States is for certain purposes as entirely the government of each state, chosen by the people thereof, and cloathed with their authority, as the government of each particular state is the government of every subdivision of that state; and no satisfactory reason has been heretofore assigned why a general rule common to all, and punishing generally the malicious calumniators of magistrates, should not be as applicable to magistrates chosen for the whole, as to those chosen for its different parts.

If then it were even true that the punishment of the printer of malicious falsehoods affected the liberty of the press, yet the act does not abridge that liberty, since it does not substitute a harsher or severer rule of punishment than that which before existed.

On points so extremely interesting, a difference of opinion will be entertained. On such occasions all parties must be expected to maintain their real opinions, but to maintain them with moderation and with decency. The will of the majority must prevail, or the republican principle is abandoned and the nation is destroyed. If upon every constitutional question which presents itself, or on every question we choose to term constitutional, the construction of the majority shall be forcibly opposed, and hostility to the government excited throughout the nation, there is an end of our domestic peace, and we may ever bid adieu to our representative government.

The legislature of Virginia has itself passed more than one unconstitutional law, but they have not been passed with an intention to violate the constitution. On being decided to be unconstitutional by the legitimate authority, they have been permitted to fall. Had the judges deemed them constitutional, they should have been maintained. The same check, nor is it a less efficient one, exists in the government of the union. The judges of the United States are as independent as the judges of the state of Virginia, nor is there any reason to believe them less wise and less virtuous. It is their province, and their duty to construe the constitution and the laws, and it cannot be doubted, but that they will perform this duty faithfully and truly. They will perform it unwarmed by political debate, uninfluenced by party zeal. Let us in the mean time seek a repeal of any acts we may disapprove, by means authorized by our happy constitution, but let us not endeavor to disseminate among our fellow citizens the most deadly hate against the government of their own creation, against the government, on the preservation of which we firmly believe the peace and liberty of America to depend, because in some respects its judgment has differed from our own.

The First Amendment Protects Criticism of the Government

Oliver Wendell Holmes

Oliver Wendell Holmes (1841–1935) was one of the most influential Supreme Court justices in U.S. history, and the justice whose legacy is most often associated with the concept of free expression. "The right to swing my fist," Holmes once wrote, "ends where the other man's nose begins." Holmes studied with some of the greatest English philosophers of the nineteenth century and applied their theories to the practice of law. His *Common Law* (1881) is a classic in legal philosophy and still widely read today. After teaching law at Harvard University and serving for twenty years as chief justice of the Supreme Court of Massachusetts, Holmes was nominated to the U.S. Supreme Court in 1902.

In 1919, Holmes definitively established his legacy as a defender of free speech. The Sedition Act of 1918, passed by the U.S. Congress as a protective measure during World War I, included a clause punishing anyone who "by word or act support[s] or favor[s] the cause of the German Empire or its allies in the present war, or by word or act oppose[s] the cause of the United States." The law was tested when Jacob Abrams, a Communist, published two pamphlets that were highly critical of U.S. foreign policy. He was arrested under the Sedition Act and sentenced to twenty years in prison. In *U.S. v. Abrams* (1919), the U.S. Supreme Court supported the verdict and found the Sedition Act to be constitutional. In the dissenting opinion,

Oliver Wendell Holmes, dissenting opinion, *U.S. v. Abrams*, 1919.

reprinted here, Justice Holmes argues that the Supreme Court's decision failed to enforce the First Amendment.

Over time, Holmes's opinion became the predominant one. In 1921, the U.S. Congress repealed the Sedition Act, and most of the people who had been punished under the act were granted clemency. Later Supreme Court rulings found similar state legislation to be unconstitutional, setting a strong precedent against future sedition acts.

As you read, consider the following questions:
1. According to Holmes, when is it acceptable to restrict speech?
2. What is Holmes's opinion of the views expressed in Abrams's pamphlets?

This indictment is founded wholly upon the publication of two leaflets which I shall describe in a moment. The first count charges a conspiracy pending the war with Germany to publish abusive language about the form of government of the United States, laying the preparation and publishing of the first leaflet as overt acts. The second count charges a conspiracy pending the war to publish language intended to bring the form of government into contempt, laying the preparation and publishing of the two leaflets as overt acts. The third count alleges a conspiracy to encourage resistance to the United States in the same war and to attempt to effectuate the purpose by publishing the same leaflets. The fourth count lays a conspiracy to incite curtailment of production of things necessary to the prosecution of the war and to attempt to accomplish it by publishing the second leaflet to which I have referred.

Two Leaflets

The first of these leaflets says that the President's cowardly silence about the intervention in Russia reveals the hypocrisy of the plutocratic gang in Washington. It intimates that 'German militarism combined with allied capitalism to crush the Russian revolution'—goes on that the tyrants of the world fight each other until they see a common enemy—working class enlightenment, when they combine to crush it; and that now militarism and capitalism combined, though not openly, to crush the Russian revolution. It says that there is only one enemy of the workers of the world and that is capitalism; that it is a crime for workers of America, etc., to fight the workers' republic of Russia, and ends 'Awake! Awake, you workers of the world! Revolutionists.' A note adds 'It is absurd to call us pro-German. We hate and despise German militarism more than do you hypocritical tyrants. We have more reason for denouncing German militarism than has the coward of the White House.'

The other leaflet, headed 'Workers—Wake Up,' with abusive language says that America together with the Allies will march for Russia to help the Czecko-Slovaks in their struggle against the Bolsheviki, and that this time the hypocrites shall not fool the Russian emigrants and friends of Russia in America. It tells the Russian emigrants that they now must spit in the face of the false military propaganda by which their sympathy and help to the prosecution of the war have been called forth and says that with the money they have lent or are going to lend 'they will make bullets not only for the Germans but also for the Workers Soviets of Russia,' and further, 'Workers in the ammunition factories, you are producing bullets, bayonets, cannon to murder not only the Germans, but also your dearest, best, who are in Russia fighting for freedom.' It then appeals to the same Russian emigrants at some length not to consent to the 'inquisitionary expedition in Russia,' and says that the destruction of the Russian revolution is 'the politics of the march on Russia.' The leaflet winds up by saying 'Workers, our reply to this barbaric intervention has to be a general strike!' and after a few words on the spirit of revolution, exhortations not to be afraid, and some usual tall talk ends 'Woe unto those who will be in the way of progress. Let solidarity live! The Rebels.'

No argument seems to be necessary to show that these pronunciamentos in no way attack the form of government of the United States, or that they do not support either of the first two counts. What little I have to say about the third count may be postponed until I have considered the fourth. With regard to that it seems too plain to be denied that the suggestion to workers in the ammunition factories that they are producing bullets to murder their dearest, and the further advocacy of a general strike, both in the second leaflet, do urge curtailment of production of things necessary to the prosecution of the war within the meaning of the [Sedition] Act of May 16, 1918, amending section 3 of the earlier [Espionage] Act of 1917. But to make the conduct criminal that statute requires that it should be 'with intent by such curtailment to cripple or hinder the United States in the prosecution of the war.' It seems to me that no such intent is proved.

A Question of Intent

I am aware of course that the word 'intent' as vaguely used in ordinary legal discussion means no more than knowledge at the time of the act that the consequences said to be intended will ensue. Even less than that will satisfy the general principle of civil and criminal liability. A man may have to pay damages, may be sent to prison, at common law might be hanged, if at the time of his act he knew facts from which common experience showed that the consequences would follow, whether he individually could foresee them or not. But, when words are used exactly, a deed is not done with intent to produce a consequence unless that consequence is the aim of the deed. It may be obvious, and obvious to the actor, that the consequence will follow, and he may be liable for it even if he regrets it, but he does not do the act with intent to produce it unless the aim to produce it is the proximate motive of the specific act, although there may be some deeper motive behind.

It seems to me that this statute must be taken to use its words in a strict and accurate sense. They would be absurd in any other. A patriot might think that we were wasting money on aeroplanes, or making more cannon of a certain kind than we needed, and might advocate curtailment with success, yet even if it turned out that the curtailment hindered and was thought by other minds to have been obviously likely to hinder the United States in the prosecution of the war, no one would hold such conduct a crime. I admit that my illustration does not answer all that might be said but it is enough to show what I think and to let me pass to a more important aspect of the case. I refer to the First Amendment to the Constitution that Congress shall make no law abridging the freedom of speech.

I never have seen any reason to doubt that the questions of law that alone were before this Court in the [Sedition] Cases of *Schenck, Frohwerk,* and *Debs* were rightly decided. I do not doubt for a moment that by the same reasoning that would justify punishing persuasion to murder, the United States constitutionally may punish speech that produces or is intended to produce a clear and imminent danger that it will bring about forthwith certain substantive evils that the United States constitutionally may seek to prevent. The power undoubtedly is greater in time of war than in time of peace because war opens dangers that do not exist at other times.

The Right to Free Speech

But as against dangers peculiar to war, as against others, the principle of the right to free speech is always the same. It is only the present danger of immediate evil or an intent to bring it about that warrants Congress in setting a limit to the expression of opinion where private rights are not concerned. Congress certainly cannot forbid all effort to change the mind of the country. Now nobody can suppose that the surreptitious publishing of a silly leaflet by an unknown man, without more, would present any immediate danger that its opinions would hinder the success of the government arms or have any appreciable tendency to do so. Publishing those opinions for the very purpose of obstructing, however, might indicate a greater danger and at any rate would have the quality of an attempt. So I assume that the second leaflet if published for the purposes alleged in the fourth count might be punishable. But it seems pretty clear to me that nothing less than that would bring these papers within the scope of this law. An actual intent in the sense that I have explained is necessary to constitute an attempt, where a further act of the same individual is required to complete the substantive crime. . . . It is necessary where the success of the attempt depends upon others because if that intent is not present the actor's aim may be accomplished without bringing about the evils sought to be checked. An intent to prevent interference with the revolution in Russia might have been satisfied without any hindrance to carrying on the war in which we were engaged.

I do not see how anyone can find the intent required by the statute in any of the defendant's words. The second leaflet is the only one that affords even a foundation for the charge, and there, without invoking the hatred of German militarism expressed in the former one, it is evident from the beginning to the end that the only object of the paper is to help Russia and stop American intervention there against the popular government—not to impede the United States in the war that it was carrying on. To say that two phrases taken literally might import a suggestion of conduct that would have interference with the war as an indirect and probably undesired effect seems to me by no means enough to show an attempt to produce that effect.

I return for a moment to the third count. That charges an intent to provoke resistance to the United States in its war with Germany. Taking the clause in the statute that deals with that in connection with the other elaborate provisions of the Act, I think that resistance to the United States means some forcible act of opposition to some proceeding of the United States in pursuance of the war. I think the intent must be the specific intent that I have described and for the reasons that I have given I think that no such intent was proved or existed in fact. I also think that there is no hint at resistance to the United States as I construe the phrase.

Freedom of Speech

In this case sentences of twenty years imprisonment have been imposed for the publishing of two leaflets that I believe the defendants had as much right to publish as the Government has to publish the Constitution of the United States now vainly invoked by them. Even if I am technically wrong and enough can be squeezed from these poor and puny anonymities to turn the color of legal litmus paper; I will add, even if what I think the necessary intent were shown; the most nominal punishment seems to me all that possible could be inflicted, unless the defendants are to be made to suffer not for what the indictment alleges but for the creed that they avow—a creed that I believe to be the creed of ignorance and immaturity when honestly held, as I see no reason to doubt that it was held here but which, although made the subject of examination at the trial, no one has a right even to consider in dealing with the charges before the Court.

Persecution for the expression of opinions seems to me perfectly logical. If you have no doubt of your premises or your power and want a certain result with all your heart you naturally express your wishes in law and sweep away all opposition. To allow opposition by speech seems to indicate that you think the speech impotent, as when a man says that he has squared the circle, or that you do not care whole heartedly for the result, or that you doubt either your power or your premises. But when men have realized that time has upset many fighting faiths, they may come to believe even more than they believe the very foundations of their own conduct that the ultimate good desired is better reached by free trade in ideas—that the best test of truth is the power of the thought to get itself accepted in the competition of the market, and that truth is the only ground upon which their wishes safely can be carried out. That at any rate is the theory of our Constitution. It is an experiment, as all life is an experiment.

Every year if not every day we have to wager our salvation upon some prophecy based upon imperfect knowledge. While that experiment is part of our system I think that we should be eternally vigilant against attempts to check the expression of opinions that we loathe and believe to be fraught with death, unless they so imminently threaten immediate interference with the lawful and pressing purposes of the law that an immediate check is required to save the country. I wholly disagree with the argument of the Government that the First Amendment left the common law as to seditious libel in force. History seems to me against the notion. I had conceived that the United States through many years had shown its repentance for the Sedition Act of 1798 by repaying fines that it imposed. Only the emergency that makes it immediately dangerous to leave the correction of evil counsels to time warrants making any exception to the sweeping command, 'Congress shall make no law abridging the freedom of speech.' Of course I am speaking only of expressions of opinion and exhortations, which were all that were uttered here, but I regret that I cannot put into more impressive words my belief that in their conviction upon this indictment the defendants were deprived of their rights under the Constitution of the United States.

Obscenity and Censorship

Anthony Comstock, interviewed by Mary Alden Hopkins

As founder of the New York Society for the Suppression of Vice, Anthony Comstock (1844–1915) waged a religious campaign against obscenity, indecency, sacrilege, and fraud. Under political pressure, the U.S. Postal Service enlisted Comstock as a special agent in 1873, granting him the authority to inspect all mail and arrest suspects without filing an arrest warrant. Comstock encouraged the U.S. Congress to pass a new postal regulation prohibiting the sending of material on contraception and abortion; he then used the broad wording of the law—which banned "any filthy, vile, or indecent thing"—to target fraud, quackery, gambling, religious free thought, and mainstream art and literature (including the novels of Theodore Dreiser and the plays of George Bernard Shaw). By the time he died in 1915, Comstock had destroyed over fifty tons of books and over 40 million photographs and drawings. He had been personally responsible for nearly four thousand arrests and, he frequently boasted, at least fifteen suicides. He was, in short, the most radically successful censor in American history.

Comstock's law influenced numerous other federal and state obscenity codes. However, in subsequent decades nearly all of Comstock's restrictions were declared to be in violation of the First Amendment. The Supreme Court established narrower obscenity standards during the 1950s and 1960s and explicitly struck down all postal bans on information pertaining to contraception in 1971.

In this interview from a 1915 issue of *Harper's Weekly*, journalist Mary Alden Hopkins asks Comstock to explain his restrictions on material having to do with abortion, contraception, and sexual health issues.

Mary Alden Hopkins, "Birth Control and Public Morals: An Interview with Anthony Comstock," *Harper's Weekly*, May 22, 1915.

As you read, consider the following questions:
1. According to Comstock, why is indecent material dangerous?
2. How does Comstock respond to critics who argue that banning educational material on contraception, abortion, and sexual health issues makes it more difficult for doctors to do their jobs?

"Have read your articles. Self control and obedience to Nature's laws, you seem to overlook. Let men and women live a life above the level of the beasts. I see nothing in either of your articles along these lines. Existing laws are an imperative necessity in order to prevent the downfall of youths of both sex," wrote Mr. Anthony Comstock, secretary of the New York Society for the Suppression of Vice, replying to my request for an interview on the subject of Birth Control.

During the interview which he kindly allowed me, he reiterated his belief in the absolute necessity of drastic laws.

"To repeal the present laws would be a crime against society," he said, "and especially a crime against young women."

A Unique Crusader
Although the name Anthony Comstock is known all over the country and over the most of the civilized world, comparatively few people know for exactly what Mr. Comstock stands and what he has accomplished. It has been the policy of those who oppose his work to speak flippantly of it and to minimize its results. The Society for the Suppression of Vice was formed to support Mr. Comstock, from the beginning he has been its driving force, and it is giving him only the credit which is due him to say that the tremendous accomplishments of the society in its fight against vicious publications for the last forty years have been in reality the accomplishments of Mr. Comstock.

Up to 1914, Mr. Comstock had caused to be arraigned in state and federal courts 3697 persons, of whom 2740 were either convicted or pleaded guilty. On these were imposed fines to the extent of $237,134.30 and imprisonments to the length of 565 years, 11 months, and 20 days.

To this remarkable record of activity can be added since that date 176 arrests and 141 convictions.

Vile Books

The story of how Mr. Comstock began his unusual profession is as interesting as the story of any of the famous captains of industry. He has, if one may borrow a stage term, "created" his unique position.

"My attention was first drawn to the publication of vile books forty-three years ago when I was a clerk here in New York City," said Mr. Comstock.

"There was in existence at that time a kind of circulating library where my fellow clerks went, made a deposit, and received the vilest of literature, and after reading it, received back the deposit or took other books. I saw young men being debauched by this pernicious influence.

"On March 2nd, 1872, I brought about the arrest of seven persons dealing in obscene books, pictures, and articles. I found that there were 169 books some of which had been in circulation since before I was born and which were publicly advertised and sold in connection with articles for producing abortion, prevention of conception, articles to aid seductions, and for indiscreet and immoral use. I had four publishers dealing in these arrested and the plates for 167 of these books destroyed. The other two books dropped out of sight. I have not seen a copy of one of them for forty years."

From this time on Mr. Comstock devoted his attention to this work, although it was, as he once said, like standing at the mouth of a sewer. Several times men whom he has arrested, have later tried to kill him.

Section 211

There were no laws covering this ostracised business at that time. In March 1873, Mr. Comstock secured the passage of stringent federal laws closing the mails and the ports to this atrocious business. Two days afterwards, upon the request of certain Senators, Mr. Comstock was appointed Special Agent of the Post Office Department to enforce these laws. He now holds the position of Post Office Inspector. The federal law as it at present stands is as follows:

United States Criminal Code, Section 211.

(Act of March 4th, 1909, Chapter 321, Section 211, United States Statutes at Large, vol. 35, part 1, page 1088 et seq.)

Every obscene, lewd, or lascivious and every filthy book, pamphlet, picture, paper, letter, writing, print, or other publication of an indecent character, and every article or thing designated, adapted or intended for preventing conception or procuring abortion, or for any indecent or immoral use; and every article, instrument, substance, drugs, medicine, or thing which is advertised or described in a manner calculated to lead another to use or apply it for preventing conception or producing abortion, or for any indecent or immoral purpose; and every written or printed card, circular, book, pamphlet, advertisement or notice or any kind giving information, directly, or indirectly, where or how, or by what means any of the hereinbefore mentioned matters, articles or things may be obtained or made, or where or by whom any act or operation of any kind for the procuring or producing of abortion will be done or performed, or how or by what means conception may be prevented or abortion produced, whether sealed or unsealed; and every letter, packet or package or other mail matter containing any filthy, vile or indecent thing, device or substance; and every paper, writing, advertisement or representation that any article, instrument, substance, drug, medicine or thing may, or can be used or applied for preventing conception or producing abortion, or for any indecent or immoral purpose; and every description calculated to induce or incite a person to so use or apply any such article, instrument, substance, drug, medicine or thing, is hereby declared to be non-mailable matter, and shall not be conveyed in the mails or delivered from any post office or by any letter carrier. Whosoever shall knowingly deposit or cause to be deposited for mailing of delivery, anything declared by this section to be non-mailable, or shall knowingly take, or cause the same to be taken, from the mails for the purpose of circulating or disposing thereof, or of aiding in the circulation or disposition of the same, shall be fined not more than $5000, or imprisoned not more than five years, or both.

Protecting Young Minds

Any one who has the patience to read through this carefully drawn law will see that it covers—well, everything. The detailed accuracy with which it is constructed partly explains Mr. Comstock's almost uniform success in securing convictions. One possible loophole suggested itself to me.

"Does it not," I asked, "allow the judge considerable leeway in deciding whether or not a book or a picture, is immoral?"

"No," replied Mr. Comstock, "the highest courts in Great Britain and the United States, have laid down the test in all such matters. What he has to decide is *whether or not it might arouse in young and inexperienced minds, lewd or libidinous thoughts.*"

In these words lies the motive of Mr. Comstock's work—the protection of children under twenty-one. If at times his ban seems to some to be too sweepingly applied it is because his faith looks forward to a time when there shall be in all the world not one object to awaken sensuous thought in the minds of young people. He expressed this sense of the terrible danger in which young people stand and his society's duty toward them in his fortieth annual report:

. . . we first of all return thanks to Almighty God, the giver of every good and perfect gift, for the opportunities of service for Him in defense of the morals of the more than forty-two million youths and children twenty-one years of age, or under, in the United States of America. His blessings upon our efforts during the past year call for profound thanksgiving to Almighty God and for grateful and loyal service in the future.

This Society in a peculiar manner is permitted to stand at a vital and strategic point where the foes to moral purity seek to concentrate their most deadly forces against the integrity of the rising generation. We have been assigned by the Great Commander to constantly face some of the most insidious and deadly forces for evil that Satan is persistently aligning against the integrity of the children of the present age.

Character-Builders

And in a letter read at the fortieth anniversary he expresses himself thus:

These are three points of special importance to be emphasized:

1. Every child is a character-builder.

2. In the heart of every child there is a chamber of imagery, memory's storehouse, the commissary department in which is received, stored up and held in reserve every good or evil influence for future requisition.

3. "Be not deceived, God is not mocked. For whatsoever a man soweth that he shall also reap." "Keep thy heart with all diligence, for out of it are the issues of life."

The three great crime-breeders of today are intemperance, gambling, and evil reading. The devil is sowing his seed for his future harvest. There is no foe so much to be dreaded as that which perverts the imagination, sears the conscience, hardens the heart, and damns the soul.

If you allow the devil to decorate the Chamber of Imagery in your heart with licentious and sensual things, you will find that he has practically thrown a noose about your neck and will forever after exert himself to draw you away from the "Lamb of God which taketh away sins of the world." You have practically put rope on memory's bell and placed the other end of the rope in the devil's hands, and, though you may will out your mind, the memory of some vile story or picture that you may have looked upon, be assured that even in your most solitary moments the devil will ring memory's bell and call up the hateful thing to turn your thoughts away from God and undermine all aspirations for holy things.

Let me emphasize one fact, supported by my nearly forty-two years of public life in fighting this particular foe. My experience leads me to the conviction that once these matters enter through the eye and ear into the chamber of imagery in the heart of the child, nothing but the grace of God can ever erase or blot it out.

Finally, brethren, "let us not be weary in well doing, for in due season we shall reap if we faint not." Raise over each of your heads the banner of the Lord Jesus Christ. Look to Him as your Commander and Leader.

"If You Open the Door . . ."

I was somewhat confused at first that Mr. Comstock should class contraceptives with pornographic objects which debauch children's fancies, for I knew that the European scientists who advocate their use have no desire at all to debauch children. When I asked Mr. Comstock about this, he replied—with scant patience of "theorizers" who do not know human nature:

"If you open the door to anything, the filth will all pour in and the degradation of youth will follow."

The federal law, which we have quoted, covers only matter sent by post. This would leave large unguarded fields were it not for the state laws. The year following the passage of the federal law, Mr. Comstock obtained the passage of drastic laws in several states, and later in all states. The New York state law reads as follows:

Section 1142 of the Penal Law:

A person who sells, lends, gives away, or in any manner exhibits or offers to sell, lend or give away, or has in his possession with intent to sell, lend or give away, or advertises, or offers for sale, loan or distribution, any instrument or article, or any recipe, drug or medicine for the prevention of conception or for causing unlawful abortion, or purporting to be for the prevention of conception, or for causing unlawful abortion, or advertises, or holds out representations that it can be so used or applied, or any such description as will be calculated to lead another to so use or apply any such article, recipe, drug, medicine or instrument, or who writes or prints, or causes to be written or printed, a card, circular, pamphlet, advertisement or notice of any kind, or gives information orally, stating when, where, how, of whom, or by what means such an instrument, article, recipe, drug or medicine can be purchased or obtained, or who manufactures any such instrument, article, recipe, drug or medicine, is guilty of a misdemeanor, and shall be liable to the same penalties as provided in section eleven hundred and forty-one of this chapter.

This punishment is a sentence of not less than ten days nor more than one year's imprisonment or a fine not less than fifty dollars or both fine and imprisonment for each offense.

"Do not these laws handicap physicians?" I asked, remembering that this criticism is sometimes made.

"They do not," replied Mr. Comstock emphatically. "No reputable physician has ever been prosecuted under these laws. Have you ever known of one?" I had not, and he continued, "Only infamous doctors who advertise or send their foul matter by mail. A reputable doctor may tell his patient in his office what is necessary, and a druggist may sell on a doctor's written prescription drugs which he would not be allowed to sell otherwise."

Abortion and Contraception
This criticism of the laws interfering with doctors is so continuously made that I asked again:

"Do the laws never thwart the doctor's work; in cases, for instance, where pregnancy would endanger a woman's life?"

Mr. Comstock replied with the strongest emphasis:

"A doctor is allowed to bring on an abortion in cases where a woman's life is in danger. And is there anything in these laws that forbids a doctor's telling a woman that pregnancy must not occur for a certain length of time or at all? Can they not use self-control? Or must they sink to the level of the beasts?"

"But," I protested, repeating an argument often brought forward, although I felt as if my persistence was somewhat placing me in the ranks of those who desire evil rather than good. "If the parents lack that self-control, the punishment falls upon the child."

"It does not," replied Mr. Comstock. "The punishment fails upon the parents. When a man and woman marry they are responsible for their children. You can't reform a family in any of these superficial ways. You have to go deep down into their minds and souls. The prevention of conception would work the greatest demoralization. God has set certain natural barriers. If you turn loose the passions and break down the fear you bring worse disaster than the war. It would debase sacred things, break down the health of women and diseminate a greater curse than the plagues and diseases of Europe."

The Right to Not Speak

Robert H. Jackson

In 1942 the West Virginia State Board of Education passed a resolution requiring that all public school students salute the flag. Students who refused to do so were expelled, and both the parent and child could subsequently be arrested under compulsory education laws. A group of parents belonging to the Jehovah's Witnesses tradition—which teaches that pledging allegiance to an inanimate object is a form of idolatry—challenged the ordinance and argued that it violated the students' First Amendment rights. In *West Virginia State Board of Education v. Barnette* (1943), the Supreme Court agreed and struck down the resolution as unconstitutional.

Here, in his majority opinion, Justice Robert H. Jackson (1892–1954) explains the Court's reasoning. Although the original challenge to the ruling was based partly on the idea of religious free exercise, Jackson argues that compulsory statements of allegiance violate the free expression clause of the First Amendment. Jackson was a Supreme Court justice from 1941 to 1954. Although he had an influential thirteen-year tenure on the Supreme Court, he is best remembered for his role as chief U.S. prosecutor during the Nuremberg war crime trials of 1945–1946, in which nineteen high-ranking Nazi officers were found guilty of atrocities committed during the Holocaust.

As you read, consider the following questions:
1. According to Jackson, what does recitation of the Pledge of Allegiance really mean?
2. According to Jackson, what role should the government play in influencing public opinion?

Robert H. Jackson, majority opinion, *West Virginia State Board of Education v. Barnette*, 1943.

The [West Virginia State] Board of Education on January 9, 1942, adopted a resolution . . . ordering that the salute to the flag become 'a regular part of the program of activities in the public schools,' that all teachers and pupils 'shall be required to participate in the salute honoring the Nation represented by the Flag; provided, however, that refusal to salute the Flag be regarded as an Act of insubordination, and shall be dealt with accordingly.' The resolution originally required the 'commonly accepted salute to the Flag' which it defined. Objections to the salute as 'being too much like Hitler's' were raised by the Parent and Teachers Association, the Boy and Girl Scouts, the Red Cross, and the Federation of Women's Clubs. Some modification appears to have been made in deference to these objections, but no concession was made to Jehovah's Witnesses. What is now required is the 'stiff-arm' salute, the saluter to keep the right hand raised with palm turned up while the following is repeated: 'I pledge allegiance to the Flag of the United States of America and to the Republic for which it stands; one Nation, indivisible, with liberty and justice for all.'

Failure to conform is 'insubordination' dealt with by expulsion. Readmission is denied by statute until compliance. Meanwhile the expelled child is 'unlawfully absent' and may be proceeded against as a delinquent. His parents or guardians are liable to prosecution, and if convicted are subject to [a] fine not exceeding $50 and jail term not exceeding thirty days.

Appellees, citizens of the United States and of West Virginia, brought suit in the United States District Court for themselves and others similarly situated asking its injunction to restrain enforcement of these laws and regulations against Jehovah's Witnesses. The Witnesses are an unincorporated body teaching that the obligation imposed by law of God is superior to that of laws enacted by temporal government. Their religious beliefs include a literal version of Exodus, Chapter 20, verses 4 and 5, which says: 'Thou shalt not make unto thee any graven image, or any likeness of anything that is in heaven above, or that is in the earth beneath, or that is in the water under the earth; thou shalt not bow down thyself to them nor serve them.' They consider that the flag is an 'image' within this command. For this reason they refuse to salute it. Children of this faith have been expelled from school and are threatened with exclusion for no other cause. Officials threaten to send them to reformatories maintained for criminally inclined juveniles. Parents of such children have been prosecuted and are threatened with prosecutions for causing delinquency. . . .

Autonomy and the State

The freedom asserted by these appellees does not bring them into collision with rights asserted by any other individual. It is such conflicts which most frequently require intervention of the State to determine where the rights of one end and those of another begin. But the refusal of these persons to participate in the ceremony does not interfere with or deny rights of others to do so. Nor is there any question in this case that their behavior is peaceable and orderly. The sole conflict is between authority and rights of the individual. The State asserts power to condition access to public education on making a prescribed sign and profession and at the same time to coerce attendance by punishing both parent and child. The latter stand on a right of self-determination in matters that touch individual opinion and personal attitude.

There is no doubt that, in connection with the pledges, the flag salute is a form of utterance. Symbolism is a primitive but effective way of communicating ideas. The use of an emblem or flag to symbolize some system, idea, institution, or personality, is a short cut from mind to mind. Causes and nations, political parties, lodges and ecclesiastical groups seek to knit the loyalty of their followings to a flag or banner, a color or design. The State announces rank, function, and authority through crowns and maces, uniforms and black robes; the church speaks through the Cross, the Crucifix, the altar and shrine, and clerical rainment. Symbols of State often convey political ideas just as religious symbols come to convey theological ones. Associated with many of these symbols are appropriate gestures of acceptance or respect: a salute, a bowed or bared head, a bended knee. A person gets from a symbol the meaning he puts into it, and what is one man's comfort and inspiration is another's jest and scorn.

Over a decade ago Chief Justice [Charles E.] Hughes led this Court in holding that the display of a red flag as a symbol of opposition by peaceful and legal means to organized government was protected by the free speech guaranties of the Constitution. Here it is the State that employs a flag as a symbol of adherence to government as presently organized. It requires the individual to communicate by word and sign his acceptance of the political ideas it thus bespeaks. Objection to this form of communication when coerced is an old one, well known to the framers of the Bill of Rights.

Allegiance and Belief

It is also to be noted that the compulsory flag salute and pledge requires affirmation of a belief and an attitude of mind. It is not clear whether the regulation contemplates that pupils forgo any contrary convictions of their own and become unwilling converts to the prescribed ceremony or whether it will be acceptable if they simulate assent by words without belief and by a gesture barren of meaning. It is now a commonplace that censorship or suppression of expression of opinion is tolerated by our Constitution only when the expression presents a clear and present danger of action of a kind the State is empowered to prevent and punish. It would seem that involuntary affirmation could be commanded only on even more immediate and urgent grounds than silence. But here the power of compulsion is invoked without any allegation that remaining passive during a flag salute ritual creates a clear and present danger that would justify an effort even to muffle expression. To sustain the compulsory flag salute we are required to say that a Bill of Rights which guards the individual's right to speak his own mind, left it open to public authorities to compel him to utter what is not in his mind.

Whether the First Amendment to the Constitution will permit officials to order observance of ritual of this nature does not depend upon whether as a voluntary exercise we would think it to be good, bad or merely innocuous. Any credo of nationalism is likely to include what some disapprove or to omit what others think essential, and to give off different overtones as it takes on different accents or interpretations. If official power exists to coerce acceptance of any patriotic creed, what it shall contain cannot be decided by courts, but must be largely discretionary with the ordaining authority, whose power to prescribe would no doubt include power to amend. Hence validity of the asserted power to force an American citizen publicly to profess any statement of belief or to engage in any ceremony of assent to one presents questions of power that must be considered independently of any idea we may have as to the utility of the ceremony in question.

Nor does the issue as we see it turn on one's possession of particular religious views or the sincerity with which they are held. While religion supplies appellees' motive for enduring the discomforts of making the issue in this case, many citizens who do not share these religious views hold such a compulsory rite to infringe constitutional liberty of the individual. It is not necessary to inquire whether nonconformist beliefs will exempt from the duty to salute unless we first find power to make the salute a legal duty. . . .

Nationalism and the First Amendment

Struggles to coerce uniformity of sentiment in support of some end thought essential to their time and country have been waged by many good as well as by evil men. Nationalism is a relatively recent phenomenon but at other times and places the ends have been racial or territorial security, support of a dynasty or regime, and particular plans for saving souls. As first and moderate methods to attain unity have failed, those bent on its accomplishment must resort to an ever-increasing severity. As governmental pressure toward unity becomes greater, so strife becomes more bitter as to whose unity it shall be. Probably no deeper division of our people could proceed from any provocation than from finding it necessary to choose what doctrine and whose program public educational officials shall compel youth to unite in embracing. Ultimate futility of such attempts to compel coherence is the lesson of every such effort from the Roman drive to stamp out Christianity as a disturber of its pagan unity, the Inquisition, as a means to religious and dynastic unity, the Siberian exiles as a means to Russian unity, down to the fast failing efforts of our present totalitarian enemies. Those who begin coercive elimination of dissent soon find themselves exterminating dissenters. Compulsory unification of opinion achieves only the unanimity of the graveyard.

It seems trite but necessary to say that the First Amendment to our Constitution was designed to avoid these ends by avoiding these beginnings. There is no mysticism in the American concept of the State or of the nature or origin of its authority. We set up government by consent of the governed, and the Bill of Rights denies those in power any legal opportunity to coerce that consent. Authority here is to be controlled by public opinion, not public opinion by authority.

The case is made difficult not because the principles of its decision are obscure but because the flag involved is our own. Nevertheless, we apply the limitations of the Constitution with no fear that freedom to be intellectually and spiritually diverse or even contrary will disintegrate the social organization. To believe that patriotism will not flourish if patriotic ceremonies are voluntary and spontaneous instead of a compulsory routine is to make an unflattering estimate of the appeal of our institutions to free minds. We can have intellectual individualism and the rich cultural diversities that we owe to exceptional minds only at the price of occasional eccentricity and abnormal attitudes. When they are so harmless to others or to the State as those we deal with here, the price is not too great. But freedom to differ is not limited to things that do not matter much. That would be a mere shadow of freedom. The test of its substance is the right to differ as to things that touch the heart of the existing order.

If there is any fixed star in our constitutional constellation, it is that no official, high or petty, can prescribe what shall be orthodox in politics, nationalism, religion, or other matters of opinion or force citizens to confess by word or act their faith therein. If there are any circumstances which permit an exception, they do not now occur to us.

3

CHURCH AND STATE

CHAPTER PREFACE

Congress shall make no law respecting an establishment of religion, or prohibiting the free exercise thereof . . .

—Amendment I

During the seventeenth century, the concepts of church-state separation and religious free exercise were alien to most American colonies. States were either explicitly affiliated with the Church of England (as Virginia was) or expressed a more radical Puritan theology (as Massachusetts did). Non-Christian religious expression was almost universally restricted, and even some minority forms of Christianity—Catholicism, for example—were restricted in most states and occasionally punished by death. Colonies were sometimes founded primarily for religious reasons: Rhode Island as a haven for Baptists, Maryland as a haven for Roman Catholics, and Pennsylvania as a haven for Quakers.

By the time of the American Revolution, the idea of state-supported religion had largely lost its appeal. The Church of England, perceived as part and parcel of the British Empire that the Americans had rebelled against, was essentially outlawed, and state bills of rights in Virginia and Massachusetts provided for individual religious liberty as a fundamental right. Nearly all influential figures working within the Constitutional Convention—both Federalist and Anti-Federalist—agreed that there should be no state-sponsored Church of the United States and that religious free exercise should be protected. The founders expressed these beliefs by passing the First Amendment to the Constitution.

Today, a great deal of disagreement exists over the precise intent of the First Amendment's church-state clause. Although few oppose the right to religious free exercise, the establishment clause—preventing the United States from funding or otherwise supporting religious institutions—has been interpreted in a number of ways. These interpretations can be classified into three basic categories: preferentialism, accommodationism, and separatism.

Church-state preferentialism holds that the establishment clause was intended to prevent an official state-run church but does not prevent Congress from supporting Christianity as a national religion. Although some conservative groups support this position, it is considered rare and is not well-represented in mainstream politics.

Church-state accommodationism is the belief that Congress has the power to accommodate, or provide special support to, religious institutions as long as it does not favor any one religious institution over another. A good example is President George W. Bush's proposed faith-based charity initiative, which would fund religious organizations but treat all faith traditions equally. Most church-state accommodationists also believe that the U.S. government can affirm specific religious beliefs, as it does in the Pledge of Allegiance ("one nation, under God") and on coins ("in God we trust"), provided that it does so in a purely ceremonial way. Most Republicans, and some Democrats, are church-state accommodationists.

Church-state separatism is the literal belief in Thomas Jefferson's "wall of separation between church and state." It holds that Congress can grant no special privileges to religion, and many church-state separatists also believe that the U.S. government should not officially affirm specific religious beliefs under any circumstances. Many Democrats, and some Republicans, are church-state separatists, and this position has historically been well represented on the Supreme Court.

One of the most controversial church-state issues is public school prayer, a topic that clearly highlights how the three traditions differ. Preferentialists, who believe that the United States is both historically and philosophically a Christian nation, support a public school prayer that specifically affirms the doctrines of Christianity. Accommodationists do not object to state-supported public school prayer, provided that it is both inclusive and optional. Separatists argue that any state-sponsored public school prayer would violate the First Amendment's religious establishment clause.

The documents in the following chapter provide differing perspectives on the issue of church-state separation.

The Freedom of Conscience

Thomas Jefferson

Thomas Jefferson (1743–1826) is best known as the author of the Declaration of Independence (1776), which grounded American legal philosophy in the concept of natural rights. Jefferson studied the philosophy of natural rights at the College of William and Mary, where he earned a degree in law and history. After serving in the U.S. Congress and Virginia legislature, Jefferson was elected governor of Virginia in 1779. When his term as governor ended in 1783, he quickly returned to the U.S. Congress and immersed himself in political work. In 1785, he was appointed ambassador to France.

It was in Paris that Jefferson's lively and opinionated *Notes on the State of Virginia* (1785) was published. In this excerpt from *Notes*, Jefferson discusses the concept of religious liberty. Jefferson felt that U.S. law ought to explicitly protect religious expression, and many scholars believe that it was Jefferson's urgent letters to the young James Madison that ultimately convinced Madison to support a bill of rights in 1789. The very first phrase in the Bill of Rights—"Congress shall make no law respecting an establishment of religion, or prohibiting the free exercise thereof"—reflects Jefferson's concerns. Later, Jefferson would suggest a complete "wall of separation between church and state."

In 1800, Thomas Jefferson became the third president of the United States.

Thomas Jefferson, *Notes on the State of Virginia*, Philadelphia: Pritchard & Hall, 1788.

As you read, consider the following questions:
1. How does Jefferson characterize the state of religious freedom in the United States?
2. According to Jefferson, what are the best antidotes to errors of thought?
3. In Jefferson's opinion, what is the single best way to silence religious disputes?

The first settlers in this country were emigrants from England, of the English church, just at a point of time when it was flushed with complete victory over the religious of all other persuasions. Possessed, as they became, of the powers of making, administering, and executing the laws, they shewed equal intolerance in this country with their Presbyterian brethren, who had emigrated to the northern government. The poor Quakers were flying from persecution in England. They cast their eyes on these new countries as asylums of civil and religious freedom; but they found them free only for the reigning sect. Several acts of the Virginia assembly of 1659, 1662, and 1693, had made it penal in parents to refuse to have their children baptized; had prohibited the unlawful assembling of Quakers; had made it penal for any master of a vessel to bring a Quaker into the state; had ordered those already here, and such as should come thereafter, to be imprisoned till they should abjure the country; provided a milder punishment for their first and second return, but death for their third; had inhibited all persons from suffering their meetings in or near their houses, entertaining them individually, or disposing of books which supported their tenets. If no capital execution took place here, as did in New-England, it was not owing to the moderation of the church, or spirit of the legislature, as may be inferred from the law itself; but to historical circumstances which have not been handed down to us. The Anglicans retained full possession of the country about a century. Other opinions began then to creep in, and the great care of the government to support their own church, having begotten an equal degree of indolence in its clergy, two-thirds of the people had become dissenters at the commencement of the present revolution [the American Revolution]. The laws indeed were still oppressive on them, but the spirit of the one party had subsided into moderation, and of the other had risen to a degree of determination which commanded respect.

Religious Oppressions Under Common Law

The present state of our laws on the subject of religion is this. The convention of May 1776, in their declaration of rights, declared it to be a truth, and a natural right, that the exercise of religion should be free; but when they proceeded to form on that declaration the ordinance of government, instead of taking up every principle declared in the bill of rights, and guarding it by legislative sanction, they passed over that which asserted our religious rights, leaving them as they found them. The same convention, however, when they met as a member of the general assembly in October 1776, repealed all *acts of parliament* which had rendered criminal the maintaining any opinions in matters of religion, the forbearing to repair to church, and the exercising any mode of worship; and suspended the laws giving salaries to the clergy, which suspension was made perpetual in October 1779. Statutory oppressions in religion being thus wiped away, we remain at present under those only imposed by the common law, or by our own acts of assembly. At the common law, *heresy* was a capital offence, punishable by burning. Its definition was left to the ecclesiastical judges, before whom the conviction was, till statute [a subsequent] circumscribed it, by declaring, that nothing should be deemed heresy, but what had been so determined by authority of the canonical scriptures, or by one of the four first general councils, or by some other council having for the grounds of their declaration the express and plain words of the scriptures. Heresy, thus circumscribed, being an offence at the common law, our act of assembly of October 1777, gives cognizance of it to the general court, by declaring, that the jurisdiction of that court shall be general in all matters at the common law. The execution is by the writ *de hæretico comburendo.* By our own [Virginia] act of assembly of 1705, if a person brought up in the Christian religion denies the being of a God, or the Trinity, or asserts there are more gods than one, or denies the Christian religion to be true, or the scriptures to be of divine authority, he is punishable on the first offence by incapacity to hold any office or employment ecclesiastical, civil, or military; on the second by disability to sue, to take any gift or legacy, to be guardian, executor, or administrator, and by three years imprisonment, without bail. A father's right to the custody of his own children being founded in law on his right of guardianship, this being taken away, they may of course be severed from him, and put by the authority of a court, into more orthodox hands. This is a summary view of that religious slavery, under which a people have been willing to remain, who have lavished their lives and fortunes for the establishment of their civil freedom.

The Benefits of Religious Free Expression
The error seems not sufficiently eradicated, that the operations of the mind, as well as the acts of the body, are subject to the coercion of the laws. But our rulers can have authority over such natural rights only as we have submitted to them. The rights of conscience we never submitted, we could not submit. We are answerable for them to our God. The legitimate powers of government extend to such acts only as are injurious to others. But it does me no injury for my neighbour to say there are twenty gods, or no god. It neither picks my pocket nor breaks my leg. If it be said, his testimony in a court of justice cannot be relied on, reject it then, and be the stigma on him. Constraint may make him worse by making him a hypocrite, but it will never make him a truer man. It may fix him obstinately in his errors, but will not cure them. Reason and free inquiry are the only effectual agents against error. Give a loose to them, they will support the true religion, by bringing every false one to

their tribunal, to the test of their investigation. They are the natural enemies of error, and of error only. Had not the Roman government permitted free inquiry, Christianity could never have been introduced. Had not free inquiry been indulged, at the æra of the reformation, the corruptions of Christianity could not have been purged away. If it be restrained now, the present corruptions will be protected, and new ones encouraged. Was the government to prescribe to us our medicine and diet, our bodies would be in such keeping as our souls are now. Thus in France the emetic was once forbidden as a medicine, and the potatoe as an article of food. Government is just as infallible too when it fixes systems in physics. Galileo was sent to the inquisition for affirming that the earth was a sphere: the government had declared it to be as flat as a

Thomas Jefferson

trencher, and Galileo was obliged to abjure his error. This error however at length prevailed, the earth became a globe, and Descartes declared it was whirled round its axis by a vortex. The government in which he lived was wise enough to see that this was no question of civil jurisdiction, or we should all have been involved by authority in vortices. In fact, the vortices have been exploded, and the Newtonian principle of gravitation is now more firmly established, on the basis of reason, than it would be were the government to step in, and to make it an article of necessary faith. Reason and experiment have been indulged, and error has fled before them. It is error alone which needs the support of government. Truth can stand by itself. Subject opinion to coercion: whom will you make your inquisitors? Fallible men; men governed by bad passions, by private as well as public reasons. And why subject it to coercion? To produce uniformity. But is uniformity of opinion desire-able? No more than of face and stature. Introduce the bed of Procrustes then, and as there is danger that the large men may beat the small, make us all of a size, by lopping the former and stretching the latter. Difference of opinion is ad-vantageous in religion. The several sects perform the office of a Censor morum over each other. Is uniformity attain-able? Millions of innocent men, women, and children, since the introduction of Christianity, have been burnt, tortured, fined, imprisoned; yet we have not advanced one inch to-wards uniformity. What has been the effect of coercion? To make one half the world fools, and the other half hyp-ocrites. To support roguery and error all over the earth. Let us reflect that it is inhabited by a thousand millions of people. That these profess probably a thousand different systems of religion. That ours is but one of that thousand. That if there be but one right, and ours that one, we should wish to see the 999 wandering sects gathered into the fold of truth. But against such a majority we cannot effect this by force. Reason and persuasion are the only practicable instruments. To make way for these, free inquiry must be indulged; and how can we wish others to indulge it while we refuse it ourselves. But every state, says an inquisitor, has established some religion. No two, say I, have estab-lished the same. Is this a proof of the infallibility of estab-lishments? Our sister states of Pennsylvania and New York, however, have long subsisted without any establishment at all. The experiment was new and doubtful when they made it. It has answered beyond conception. They flourish infi-nitely. Religion is well supported; of various kinds, indeed, but all good enough; all sufficient to preserve peace and or-der: or if a sect arises, whose tenets would subvert morals, good sense has fair play, and reasons and laughs it out of doors, without suffering the state to be troubled with it. They do not hang more malefactors than we do. They are not more disturbed with religious dissensions. On the con-trary, their harmony is unparalleled, and can be ascribed to nothing but their unbounded tolerance, because there is no other circumstance in which they differ from every nation on earth. They have made the happy discovery, that the way to silence religious disputes, is to take no notice of them. Let us too give this experiment fair play, and get rid, while we may, of those tyrannical laws. It is true, we are as yet secured against them by the spirit of the times. I doubt whether the people of this country would suffer an execution for heresy, or a three years imprisonment for not comprehending the mysteries of the Trinity. But is the spirit of the people an infallible, a permanent reliance? Is it government? Is this the kind of protection we receive in return for the rights we give up? Besides, the spirit of the times may alter, will alter. Our rulers will become corrupt, our people careless. A single zealot may commence persecutor, and better men be his victims. It can never be too often repeated, that the time for fixing every essential right on a legal basis is while our rulers are honest, and ourselves united. From the conclusion of this war we shall be going down hill. It will not then be necessary to resort every moment to the people for support. They will be forgotten, therefore, and their rights disregarded. They will forget themselves, but in the sole faculty of making money, and will never think of uniting to effect a due respect for their rights. The shackles, therefore, which shall not be knocked off at the conclusion of this war, will remain on us long, will be made heavier and heavier, till our rights shall revive or expire in a convulsion.

Why Church and State Should Work Together

Edmund Burke

Edmund Burke (1729–1797), often called the "father of conservatism," was a British political philosopher who sought gradual reform while defending his country's traditions against radical revolutionary ideals. His political career began when he entered Parliament in 1766. There he gained a reputation as a courageous advocate for the oppressed, working to improve the treatment of Britain's Roman Catholic minority and support a lenient policy toward American colonists. He made several attempts to convince the British Parliament to cede greater independence to the Americans, but was ultimately unsuccessful.

Burke's commitment to the preservation of tradition led him to condemn the French Revolution of 1789, which was directed against both the aristocracy and the clergy. In this excerpt from his *Reflections on the Revolution in France* (1790), Burke defends the concept of church-state unity. He argues that the two institutions have a natural and proper alliance and that linking the two can have substantial practical benefits.

Although some American colonists shared Burke's views regarding church and state, the establishment clause of the First Amendment served to prevent a Burkean model of church-state unity in the United States.

As you read, consider the following questions:
1. According to Burke, is religious establishment essential to political stability? Why or why not?

Edmund Burke, *Reflections on the Revolution in France*. London: J. Dodsley, 1790.

2. Why does Burke believe that a strong national church can improve political leadership?
3. According to Burke, why can't a perfect democracy be trusted to exercise sound moral judgment?

We know, and what is better we feel inwardly, that religion is the basis of civil society, and the source of all good—and of all comfort. In England we are so convinced of this, that there is no rust of superstition, with which the accumulated absurdity of the human mind might have crusted it over in the course of ages, that ninety-nine in a hundred of the people of England would not prefer to impiety. We shall never be such fools as to call in an enemy to the substance of any system to remove its corruptions, to supply its defects, or to perfect its construction. If our religious tenets should ever want a further elucidation, we shall not call on atheism to explain them. We shall not light up our temple from that unhallowed fire. It will be illuminated with other lights. It will be perfumed with other incense, than the infectious stuff which is imported by the smugglers of adulterated metaphysics. If our ecclesiastical establishment should want a revision, it is not avarice or rapacity, public or private, that we shall employ for the audit, or receipt, or application of its consecrated revenue.—Violently condemning neither the Greek nor the Armenian, nor, since heats are subsided, the Roman system of religion, we prefer the Protestant; not because we think it has less of the Christian religion in it, but because, in our judgment, it has more. We are protestants, not from indifference but from zeal.

We know, and it is our pride to know, that man is by his constitution a religious animal; that atheism is against, not only our reason but our instincts; and that it cannot prevail long. But if, in the moment of riot, and in a drunken delirium from the hot spirit drawn out of the alembick of hell, which in France is now so furiously boiling, we should uncover our nakedness by throwing off that Christian religion which has hitherto been our boast and comfort, and one great source of civilization amongst us, and among many other nations, we are apprehensive (being well aware that the mind will not endure a void) that some uncouth, pernicious, and degrading supersition, might take place of it.

For that reason, before we take from our establishment the natural human means of estimation, and give it up to contempt, as you [the French] have done, and in doing it have incurred the penalties you well deserve to suffer, we desire that some other may be presented to us in the place of it. We shall then form our judgment.

The Church as Sustainer of Culture

On these ideas, instead of quarrelling with establishments, as some do, who have made a philosophy and a religion of their hostility to such institutions, we cleave closely to them. We are resolved to keep an established church, an established monarchy, an established aristocracy, and an established democracy, each in the degree it exists, and in no greater. . . .

It has been the misfortune (not as these gentlemen think it, the glory) of this age, that every thing is to be discussed, as if the constitution of our country were to be always a subject rather of altercation than enjoyment. For this reason, as well as for the satisfaction of those among you (if any such you have among you) who may wish to profit of examples, I venture to trouble you with a few thoughts upon each of these establishments. I do not think they were unwise in ancient Rome, who, when they wished to new-model their laws, sent commissioners to examine the best constituted republics within their reach.

First, I beg leave to speak of our church establishment, which is the first of our prejudices, not a prejudice destitute of reason, but involving in it profound and extensive wisdom. I speak of it first. It is first, and last, and midst in our minds. For, taking ground on that religious system, of which we are now in possession, we continue to act on the early received, and uniformly continued sense of mankind. That sense not only, like a wise architect, hath built up the august fabric of states, but like a provident proprietor, to preserve the structure from prophanation and ruin, as a sacred temple, purged from all the impurities of fraud, and violence, and injustice, and tyranny, hath solemnly and for ever consecrated the commonwealth, and all that officiate in it. This consecration is made, that all who administer in the government of men, in which they stand in the person of God himself, should have high and worthy notions of their function and destination; that their hope should be full of immortality; that they should not look to the paltry pelf of the moment, nor to the temporary and transient praise of the vulgar, but to a solid, permanent existence, in the permanent part of their nature, and to a permanent fame and glory, in the example they leave as a rich inheritance to the world.

Such sublime principles ought to be infused into persons of exalted situations; and religious establishments provided, that may continually revive and enforce them. Every sort of moral, every sort of civil, every sort of politic institution, aiding the rational and natural ties that connect the human understanding and affections to the divine, are not more than necessary, in order to build up that wonderful structure, Man; whose prerogative it is, to be in a great degree a creature of his own making, and who when made as he ought to be made, is destined to hold no trivial place in the creation. But whenever man is put over men, as the better nature ought ever to preside, in that case more particularly, he should as nearly as possible be approximated to his perfection.

A "Wholesome Awe"
The consecration of the state, by a state religious establishment, is necessary also to operate with an wholesome awe upon free citizens; because, in order to secure their freedom, they must enjoy some determinate portion of power. To them therefore a religion connected with the state, and with their duty towards it, becomes even more necessary than in such societies, where the people by the terms of their subjection are confined to private sentiments, and the

management of their own family concerns. All persons possessing any portion of power ought to be strongly and awefully impressed with an idea that they act in trust; and that they are to account for their conduct in that trust to the one great master, author and founder of society.

This principle ought even to be more strongly impressed upon the minds of those who compose the collective sovereignty than upon those of single princes. Without instruments, these princes can do nothing. Whoever uses instruments, in finding helps, finds also impediments. Their power is therefore by no means compleat; nor are they safe in extreme abuse. Such persons, however elevated by flattery, arrogance, and self-opinion, must be sensible that, whether covered or not by positive law, in some way or other they are accountable even here for the abuse of their trust. If they are not cut off by a rebellion of their people, they may be strangled by the very Janissaries kept for their security against all other rebellion. Thus we have seen the king of France sold by his soldiers for an encrease of pay. But where popular authority is absolute and unrestrained, the people have an infinitely greater, because a far better founded confidence in their own power. They are themselves, in a great measure, their own instruments. They are nearer to their objects. Besides, they are less under responsibility to one of the greatest controlling powers on earth, the sense of fame and estimation. The share of infamy that is likely to fall to the lot of each individual in public acts, is small indeed; the operation of opinion being in the inverse ratio to the number of those who abuse power. Their own approbation of their own acts has to them the appearance of a public judgment in their favour. A perfect democracy is therefore the most shameless thing in the world. As it is the most shameless, it is also the most fearless. No man apprehends in his person he can be made subject to punishment. Certainly the people at large never ought: for as all punishments are for example towards the conservation of the people at large, the people at large can never become the subject of punishment by any human hand. It is therefore of infinite importance that they should not be suffered to imagine that their will, any more than that of kings, is the standard of right and wrong.

They ought to be persuaded that they are full as little entitled, and far less qualified, with safety to themselves, to use any arbitrary power whatsoever; that therefore they are not, under a false shew of liberty, but, in truth, to exercise an unnatural inverted domination, tyrannically to exact, from those who officiate in the state, not an entire devotion to their interest, which is their right, but an abject submission to their occasional will; extinguishing thereby, in all those who serve them, all moral principle, all sense of dignity, all use of judgment, and all consistency of character, whilst by the very same process they give themselves up a proper, a suitable, but a most contemptible prey to the servile ambition of popular sycophants or courtly flatterers.

Eternal Law and Eternal Justice

When the people have emptied themselves of all the lust of selfish will, which without religion it is utterly impossible they ever should, when they are conscious that they exercise, and exercise perhaps in an higher link of the order of delegation, the power, which to be legitimate must be according to that eternal immutable law, in which will and reason are the same, they will be more careful how they place power in base and incapable hands. In their nomination to office, they will not appoint to the exercise of authority, as to a pitiful job, but as to an holy function; not according to their sordid selfish interest, nor to their wanton caprice, nor to their arbitrary will; but they will confer that power (which any man may well tremble to give or to receive) on those only, in whom they may discern that predominant proportion of active virtue and wisdom, taken together and fitted to the charge, such, as in the great and inevitable mixed mass of human imperfections and infirmities, is to be found.

When they are habitually convinced that no evil can be acceptable, either in the act or the permission, to him whose essence is good, they will be better able to extirpate out of the minds of all magistrates, civil, ecclesiastical, or military, any thing that bears the least resemblance to a proud and lawless domination.

But one of the first and most leading principles on which the commonwealth and the laws are consecrated, is lest the temporary possessors and life-renters in it, unmindful of what they have received from their ancestors, or of what is due to their posterity, should act as if they were the entire masters; that they should not think it amongst their rights to cut off the entail, or commit waste on the inheritance, by destroying at their pleasure the whole original fabric of their society; hazarding to leave to those who come after them, a ruin instead of an habitation—and teaching these successors as little to respect their contrivances, as they had themselves respected the institutions of their forefathers. By this unprincipled facility of changing the state as often, and as much, and in as many ways as there are floating fancies or fashions, the whole chain and continuity of the commonwealth would be broken. No one generation could link with the other. Men would become little better than the flies of a summer.

The Dangers of Theocracy

Joseph Priestley

The First Amendment to the U.S. Constitution prevents the American government from establishing a national religion or state-funded church. When the amendment was first drafted in 1789, the concept of church-state separation was a fairly radical one. The vast majority of nations favored one religious tradition on an official basis. When the American colonists revolted against the Church of England (which opposed American independence), the question arose as to whether the United States should establish its own national church. When Edmund Burke proposed in his *Reflections on the Revolution in France* (1790) that every nation ought to have some sort of religious establishment, he was confronted with numerous advocates for the First Amendment's separation of church and state. One of the most vocal and well known was Joseph Priestley (1733–1804).

Priestley proposed a completely secular government, an idea that was fairly unpopular in Great Britain during his lifetime. In this excerpt from his *Essay on the First Principles of Government* (1768), Priestley provides a point-by-point critique of church-state unity, which he describes as awkward and dangerous.

As a scientist, Priestley discovered nine gases (including oxygen, ammonia, and carbon dioxide) and pioneered the field of electrothermal engineering. As a minister and theologian, he was the single person most responsible for bringing the liberal Unitarian religious movement to the United States. As a philosopher, he was regarded as one of the most prominent figures of the English Enlightenment

Joseph Priestley, *Essay on the First Principles of Government*. London: J. Johnson, 1771.

and, as a political philosopher, an early supporter of the American Revolution.

In his *Letters to the Right Honourable Edmund Burke* (1791), a response to Burke's *Reflections on the Revolution in France*, Priestley defends the French Revolution. This publication earned him both honorary French citizenship and the wrath of many of his countrymen, who burned down his home and laboratory. Faced with constant threats and harassment at home, he was welcomed to the United States in 1794 and remained popular there for the rest of his life.

As you read, consider the following questions:
1. What are Priestley's main arguments against church-state unity?
2. According to Priestley, how does the relationship between government and religion in eighteenth-century Europe differ from that of ancient Greece?
3. How does Priestley answer critics who argue that organized religion needs political support in order to survive?

The friends and advocates for church power, generally found their system on the necessity of establishing some religion or other, agreeably, they say, to the custom of all wise nations. This being admitted, it is evident, they think, that the supreme civil magistrate must have the choice of this religion, and being thus lodged in the hands of the chief magistrate, it is easily and effectually guarded. Thus the propriety of a most rigid *intolerance*, and the most abject *passive obedience* are presently, and clearly inferred; so that the people have no right to relieve themselves from ecclesiastical oppressions, except by petition to their temporal and spiritual governors, whose interest it generally is to continue every abuse that the people can complain of.

The Case Against Religious Establishment
But before this admirably connected system can be admitted, a few things should be previously considered. And I am

aware that, if they had been duly attended to, the system either would never have taken place, or it would have been so moderated, when put into execution, as that it would never have been worth the while of its advocates to contend so zealously for it.

1. All the rational plea for ecclesiastical establishments, is founded on the necessity of them, in order to enforce obedience to civil laws; but though religious considerations be allowed to be an excellent *aid* to civil sanctions, it will not, therefore, follow, as some would gladly have it understood, that, therefore, the business of civil government could not have been carried on *at all* without them. I do not know how it is, that this position seems, in general, to have passed without dispute or examination; but, for my own part, I see no reason to think that civil society could not have subsisted, and even have subsisted very well, without the aid of any foreign sanctions. I am even satisfied that, in many countries, the junction of civil and ecclesiastical powers hath done much mischief, and that it would have been a great blessing to the bulk of the people, if their magistrates had never interfered in matters of religion at all, but had left them to provide for themselves in that respect, as they generally do, with regard to medicine.

"There are," says the Bishop of Gloucester, "a numerous set of duties of *imperfect obligation*, which human laws could not reach. This can only be done by an ecclesiastical jurisdiction, intrusted by the state with coercive power. And indeed the supplying that defect, which these courts do supply, was the original and fundamental motive of the state seeking this alliance." But I would ask, Are not ecclesiastical officers *men*, mere human beings, possessed of only a limited power of discernment, as well as civil officers? Will they not, therefore, find themselves under the same difficulty in enforcing the duties of imperfect obligation, that the civil officers would have done, notwithstanding the coercive power they receive from the state for that purpose? In short, I do not see what an ecclesiastical court can do in this case, more than a civil court of equity. Is not this, in fact, confessed by this author, when he allows that "there must be an appeal from these courts to the civil, in all cases." For, if the civil courts be qualified to judge of these things, by appeal, why could they not have done it in the first instance?

2. If the expediency of ecclesiastical establishments be allowed, it is allowed on account of their *utility* only; and therefore, as there are infinite differences in the coercive power of these establishments, this reason will not justify their being carried to a greater extent than the good of society requires. And though it may be productive of, or, at least, consistent with the good of society, that the civil magistrate should give some degree of countenance to the professors of one sect of religion (which, with me, however, is extremely problematical) it were a gross perversion of all reasoning and common sense, to infer from thence, that the people should not have free liberty to dissent from this religion of their civil governor, or even to use any honest and fair method of gaining converts to what they should think to be the truth. Because whatever utility there may be in *ecclesiastical establishments*, there is certainly utility in *truth*, especially moral and religious truth; and truth can never have a fair chance of being discovered, or propagated, without the most perfect freedom of inquiry and debate.

Religion and Utility

Though it may be true, that there never was any country without some national religion, it is not true that these religions were always adopted with a view to aid the civil government. It appears to me that, with respect to the states of Greece, and other barbarous nations (for the Greeks were no better than their neighbours in this respect) motives of a very different nature from these; motives derived from nothing but the most blind and abject superstition, and the most groundless apprehensions, were those that really induced them to make such rigid provision for the perpetuity of their several religions. Their laws have not, in fact, any such intermixture of civil and religious matters, as is now found in the systems of European states. We do not find in them, that duties properly religious are enforced by civil sanctions, nor duties properly civil enforced by religious ones, in the senses in which we now use those terms, as if these things had, naturally, so necessary a connection. But in these ignorant and superstitious ages, men fancied there was what we should call an *arbitrary connection* between the observance of certain religious rites, and the continuance of certain states; and that the gods, who were particularly attentive to their preservation, would withdraw their protection, upon the disuse of those ceremonies.

The Bishop of Gloucester seems to agree with me in this, for he says, "The unity of the object of faith, and conformity to a formulary of dogmatic theology, as the terms of communion, is the great foundation and bond of religious society. Now this the several societies of pagan religion wanted, in which there was only a conformity in national ceremonies."

Had the ancient heathens entertained any such notion of the *direct* subserviency of religion to civil policy (*i.e.* in a *moral view*) as the advocates for church power endeavour to avail themselves of at this day, they would have made a distinction among religions. Whereas, it is plain they had no idea of the excellence of one mode of religion above another, as more conducive to the happiness of mankind (unless there was something peculiarly shocking in some of their rites, as that of sacrificing human victims) but they imagined that different rites, rites differing not in moral excellence, but in mere form, were necessary for different states; and that it was wrong, and hazardous, for two nations to interchange their religions.

Indeed, after these establishments had taken place, it is probable that some of the defenders of them, in ransacking their imaginations for arguments, might hit upon some such reasons as modern high churchmen have urged; but it no more follows from thence, that the establishments were originally founded on those principles, than that because plausible reasons may (for any thing I know) be alleged for the use of a *white surplice* in reading the prayers of the church, and for bishops wearing *mitres* and *lawn sleeves* [gown sleeves], that, therefore, Jesus Christ and his apostles used them.

4. Though there may be no Christian country in which some species of Christianity is not, more or less, established, *i.e.* more or less favoured by the government; yet there are countries in which less favour is shown to the prevailing mode than in others, and in which much less care is taken to guard it, as in Holland, Russia, Pensilvania, and I believe others of our American colonies. Now, let an enquiry be made into the state of these countries, and see whether the result of it will be favourable, or unfavourable to establishments. What *tendency to inconvenience* has there been observed in those states in which church government is most relaxed, and what *superior advantages*, in point of real happiness, are enjoyed in those countries in which it is strained to the highest pitch. I have no doubt of the result of such an inquiry turning out greatly in favour of the relaxation of religious establishments, if not of their total suppression. A just view of all the real evils that attend the ecclesiastical establishment in England, with respect to *knowledge, virtue, commerce*, and many other things with which the happiness of states is connected, but more especially with respect to *liberty*, would be sufficient to deter any legislator from introducing any thing like it into a new state; unless, without thinking at all, he took it for granted that there was no doing without one, or was so weak as to be frighted by the mere clamour of bigots.

Establishment and Origin

5. Though it may be true, that inconvenience would arise from the immediate suppression of religious establishments, it doth not therefore follow, that they were either necessary or expedient; that the nation would have been in a worse state if they had never existed; and that no measures ought to be taken to relax or dissolve them. . . .

Customs, of whatever kind, that have prevailed so long

as to have influenced the genius and manners of a whole nation, cannot be changed without trouble. Such a shock to men's prejudices would necessarily give them pain, and unhinge them for a time. It is the same with vicious habits of the body, which terminate in diseases and death; but must they be indulged, and the fatal consequences calmly expected, because the patient would find it painful and difficult to alter his method of living? Ecclesiastical establishments, therefore, may be a real *evil*, and a disease in civil society, and a dangerous one too, notwithstanding all the arguments for the support of them, derived from the confusion and inconvenience attending their dissolution; so far is this consideration from proving them to be things excellent or useful in themselves.

Does Religion Need the State?

Even the mischiefs that might be apprehended from attempts to amend or dissolve establishments, are much aggravated by writers. Much less opposition, I am persuaded, would arise from the source of real *bigotry*, than from the quarter of *interest*, and the bigotry that was set in motion by persons who were not themselves bigots.

It is imagined by some, that Christianity could not have subsisted without the aid of the civil powers, and that the dissolution of its establishment would endanger its very being. The Bishop of Gloucester, says, that "the state was induced to seek an alliance with the church, as the necessary means of preserving the being of religion;" and that "all the advantage the church expects from the alliance with the state, can be no other than security from all outward violence;" "it being impertinent," as he justly observes, "in the church to aim at riches, honours, and power; because these are things which, as a church, she can neither use, nor receive profit from." He also says, "that religion could not operate for want of a common arbiter, who had impartiality to apply the rule of right, and power to enforce its operations." But these persons seem not to be acquainted with its proper *internal strength*, or they would not lay so much stress on such poor and heterogeneous supports. They should consider how the Christian religion was supported, without the help of any establishment, before the time of Constantine. Is it not true, in fact, that it not only subsisted, but amazingly increased in all that period; when it was so far from being protected by civil authority, that all human powers were combined against it?

If they say it was supported by miracles in all that interval, it behoves them to make good the assertion. On the contrary, it appears from church history, that when Christianity was once established, (if I may use that term) by the preaching and miracles of the apostles, it was able afterwards to support itself by its own evidence. And this evidence is still sufficient to support it, though all the powers on earth, and the gates of hell, were combined against it. Certainly those who make use of this plea for Christian establishments seem to insinuate, that Christianity is destitute of *sufficient evidence;* and could not advance any thing more favourable to the purpose of its most inveterate enemies.

Faculty-Led Public School Prayer Violates the First Amendment

Hugo Black

Former U.S. senator Hugo Black (1886–1971) served as a justice of the Supreme Court from 1937 to 1971. A former Ku Klux Klan member, Black surprised many by becoming one of the most outspoken and influential civil rights advocates on the Supreme Court. During his tenure, he was also a staunch defender of the First Amendment.

In 1962, the school board of Hyde Park, New York, voted to begin each school day with a nondenominational prayer. Although individual participation in the prayer was theoretically voluntary, the prayer session was a required part of each morning's school schedule. Outraged parents asked the U.S. Supreme Court to review the policy's constitutionality. In *Engel v. Vitale* (1962), the Court declared that the government-mandated prayer violated the First Amendment by promoting the establishment of religion. In this excerpt from his majority opinion, Justice Hugo Black explains the Court's reasoning.

In the decades since the ruling, public school prayer has remained a controversial topic; many attempts have been made to reintroduce it. So far, none of these attempts have been successful.

As you read, consider the following questions:
1. How does Black describe the relationship between the government and religion in U.S. history?

Hugo Black, majority opinion, *Engel v. Vitale*, 1962.

2. According to Black, what is the primary danger of government-sanctioned prayer?
3. What defense does Black offer against criticism that strict application of the establishment clause is antireligious?

The respondent Board of Education of Union Free School District No. 9, New Hyde Park, New York, acting in its official capacity under state law, directed the School District's principal to cause the following prayer to be said aloud by each class in the presence of a teacher at the beginning of each school day:

> Almighty God, we acknowledge our dependence upon Thee, and we beg Thy blessings upon us, our parents, our teachers and our Country.

This daily procedure was adopted on the recommendation of the State Board of Regents, a governmental agency created by the State Constitution to which the New York Legislature has granted broad supervisory, executive, and legislative powers over the State's public school system. These state officials composed the prayer which they recommended and published as a part of their "Statement on Moral and Spiritual Training in the Schools," saying: "We believe that this Statement will be subscribed to by all men and women of good will, and we call upon all of them to aid in giving life to our program."

Shortly after the practice of reciting the Regents' prayer was adopted by the School District, the parents of ten pupils brought this action in a New York State Court insisting that use of this official prayer in the public schools was contrary to the beliefs, religions, or religious practices of both themselves and their children. Among other things, these parents challenged the constitutionality of both the state law authorizing the School District to direct the use of prayer in public schools and the School District's regulation ordering the recitation of this particular prayer on the ground that these actions of official governmental agencies violate that part of the First Amendment of the Federal Constitution which commands that "Congress shall make no law respecting an establishment of religion"—a command which was "made applicable to the State of New York by the Fourteenth Amendment of the said Constitution." The New York Court of Appeals, over the dissents of Judges Dye and Fuld, sustained an order of the lower state courts which had upheld the power of New York to use the Regents' prayer as a part of the daily procedures of its public schools so long as the schools did not compel any pupil to join in the prayer over his or his parents' objection. We granted certiorari to review this important decision involving rights protected by the First and Fourteenth Amendments.

Prayer and Religious Establishment

We think that by using its public school system to encourage recitation of the Regents' prayer, the State of New York has adopted a practice wholly inconsistent with the Establishment Clause. There can, of course, be no doubt that New York's program of daily classroom invocation of God's blessings as prescribed in the Regents' prayer is a religious activity. It is a solemn avowal of divine faith and supplication for the blessings of the Almighty. The nature of such a prayer has always been religious, none of the respondents has denied this and the trial court expressly so found:

> The religious nature of prayer was recognized by Jefferson and has been concurred in by theological writers, the United States Supreme Court and State courts and administrative officials, including New York's Commissioner of Education. A committee of the New York Legislature has agreed.

> The Board of Regents as amicus curiae, the respondents and intervenors all concede the religious nature

of prayer, but seek to distinguish this prayer because it is based on our spiritual heritage. . . .

The petitioners contend among other things that the state laws requiring or permitting use of the Regents' prayer must be struck down as a violation of the Establishment Clause because that prayer was composed by governmental officials as a part of a governmental program to further religious beliefs. For this reason, petitioners argue, the State's use of the Regents' prayer in its public school system breaches the constitutional wall of separation between Church and State. We agree with that contention since we think that the constitutional prohibition against laws respecting an establishment of religion must at least mean that in this country it is no part of the business of government to compose official prayers for any group of the American people to recite as a part of a religious program carried on by government.

It is a matter of history that this very practice of establishing governmentally composed prayers for religious services was one of the reasons which caused many of our early colonists to leave England and seek religious freedom in America. The *Book of Common Prayer*, which was created under governmental direction and which was approved by Acts of Parliament in 1548 and 1549, set out in minute detail the accepted form and content of prayer and other religious ceremonies to be used in the established, tax-supported Church of England. The controversies over the *Book* and what should be its content repeatedly threatened to disrupt the peace of that country as the accepted forms of prayer in the established church changed with the views of the particular ruler that happened to be in control at the time. Powerful groups representing some of the varying religious views of the people struggled among themselves to impress their particular views upon the Government and obtain amendments of the *Book* more suitable to their respective notions of how religious services should be conducted in order that the official religious establishment would advance their particular religious beliefs. Other groups, lacking the necessary political power to influence the Government on the matter, decided to leave England and its established church and seek freedom in America from England's governmentally ordained and supported religion.

It is an unfortunate fact of history that when some of the very groups which had most strenuously opposed the established Church of England found themselves sufficiently in control of colonial governments in this country to write their own prayers into law, they passed laws making their own religion the official religion of their respective colonies. Indeed, as late as the time of the Revolutionary War, there were established churches in at least eight of the thirteen former colonies and established religions in at least four of the other five. But the successful Revolution against English political domination was shortly followed by intense opposition to the practice of establishing religion by law. This opposition crystallized rapidly into an effective political force in Virginia where the minority religious groups such as Presbyterians, Lutherans, Quakers and Baptists had gained such strength that the adherents to the established Episcopal Church were actually a minority themselves. In 1785–1786, those opposed to the established Church, led by James Madison and Thomas Jefferson, who, though themselves not members of any of these dissenting religious groups, opposed all religious establishments by law on grounds of principle, obtained the enactment of the famous "Virginia Bill for Religious Liberty" by which all religious groups were placed on an equal footing so far as the State was concerned. Similar though less far-reaching legislation was being considered and passed in other States.

By the time of the adoption of the Constitution, our history shows that there was a widespread awareness among many Americans of the dangers of a union of Church and State. These people knew, some of them from bitter personal experience, that one of the greatest dangers to the freedom of the individual to worship in his own way lay in the Government's placing its official stamp of approval upon one particular kind of prayer or one particular form of religious services. They knew the anguish, hardship and bitter strife that could come when zealous religious groups struggled with one another to obtain the Government's stamp of approval from each King, Queen, or Protector that came to temporary power. The Constitution was intended to avert a part of this danger by leaving the government of this country in the hands of the people rather than in the hands of any monarch. But this safeguard was not enough. Our Founders were no more willing to let the content of their prayers and their privilege of praying whenever they pleased be influenced by the ballot box than they were to let these vital matters of personal conscience depend upon the succession of monarchs. The First Amendment was added to the Constitution to stand as a guarantee that neither the power nor the prestige of the Federal Government would be used to control, support or influence the kinds of prayer the American people can say—that the people's religions must not be subjected to the pressures of government for change each time a new political administration is elected to office. Under that Amendment's prohibition against governmental establishment of religion, as reinforced by the provisions of the Fourteenth Amendment, government in this country, be it state or federal, is without power to prescribe by law any particular form of prayer which is to be used as an official prayer in carrying on any program of governmentally sponsored religious activity.

A Religion of the State

There can be no doubt that New York's state prayer program officially establishes the religious beliefs embodied in the Regents' prayer. The respondents' argument to the contrary, which is largely based upon the contention that the Regents' prayer is " non-denominational" and the fact that the program, as modified and approved by state courts, does not require all pupils to recite the prayer but permits those who wish to do so to remain silent or be excused from the room, ignores the essential nature of the program's constitutional defects. Neither the fact that the prayer may be denominationally neutral nor the fact that its observance on the part of the students is voluntary can serve to free it from the limitations of the Establishment Clause, as it might from the Free Exercise Clause, of the First Amendment, both of which are operative against the States by virtue of the Fourteenth Amendment. Although these two clauses may in certain instances overlap, they forbid two quite different kinds of governmental encroachment upon religious freedom. The Establishment Clause, unlike the Free Exercise Clause, does not depend upon any showing of direct governmental compulsion and is violated by the enactment of laws which establish an official religion whether those laws operate directly to coerce nonobserving individuals or not. This is not to say, of course, that laws officially prescribing a particular form of religious worship do not involve coercion of such individuals. When the power, prestige and financial support of government is placed behind a particular religious belief, the indirect coercive pressure upon religious minorities to conform to the prevailing officially approved religion is plain. But the purposes underlying the Establishment Clause go much further than that. Its first and most immediate purpose rested on the belief that a union of government and religion tends to destroy government and to degrade religion. The history of governmentally established religion, both in England and in this country, showed that whenever government had allied itself with one particular form of religion, the inevitable result had been that it had incurred the hatred, disrespect and even contempt of those who held contrary beliefs. That same history showed that many people had lost their respect for any religion that had relied upon the support of government to spread its faith. The Establishment Clause thus stands as an expression of principle on the part of the Founders of our Constitution that religion is too personal, too sacred, too holy, to permit [in the words of James Madison] its "unhallowed perversion" by a civil magistrate. Another purpose of the Establishment Clause rested upon an awareness of the historical fact that governmentally established religions and religious persecutions go hand in hand. The Founders knew that only a few years after the *Book of Common Prayer* became the only accepted form of religious services in the established Church of England, an Act of Uniformity was passed to compel all Englishmen to attend those services and to make it a criminal offense to conduct or attend religious gatherings of any other kind—a law which was consistently flouted by dissenting religious groups in England and which contributed to widespread persecutions of people like John Bunyan who persisted in holding "unlawful [religious] meetings . . . to the great disturbance and distraction of the good subjects of this kingdom. . . ." And they knew that similar persecutions had received the sanction of law in several of the colonies in this country soon after the establishment of official religions in those colonies. It was in large part to get completely away from this sort of systematic religious persecution that the Founders brought into being our Nation, our Constitution, and our Bill of Rights with its prohibition against any governmental establishment of religion. The New York laws officially prescribing the Regents' prayer are inconsistent both with the purposes of the Establishment Clause and with the Establishment Clause itself.

It has been argued that to apply the Constitution in such a way as to prohibit state laws respecting an establishment of religious services in public schools is to indicate a hostility toward religion or toward prayer. Nothing, of course, could be more wrong. The history of man is inseparable from the history of religion. And perhaps it is not too much to say that since the beginning of that history many people have devoutly believed that "More things are wrought by prayer than this world dreams of." It was doubtless largely due to men who believed this that there grew up a sentiment that caused men to leave the cross-currents of officially established state religions and religious persecution in Europe and come to this country filled with the hope that they could find a place in which they could pray when they pleased to the God of their faith in the language they chose. And there were men of this same faith in the power of prayer who led the fight for adoption of our Constitution and also for our Bill of Rights with the very guarantees of religious freedom that forbid the sort of governmental activity which New York has attempted here. These men knew that the First Amendment, which tried to put an end to governmental control of religion and of prayer, was not written to destroy either. They knew rather that it was written to quiet well-justified fears which nearly all of them felt arising out of an awareness that governments of the past had shackled men's tongues to make them speak only the religious thoughts that government wanted them to speak and to pray only to the God that government wanted them to pray to. It is neither sacrilegious nor antireligious to say that each separate government in this country should stay out of the business of writing or sanctioning official prayers and leave that purely religious function to the people themselves and to those the people choose to look to for religious guidance.

It is true that New York's establishment of its Regents' prayer as an officially approved religious doctrine of that State does not amount to a total establishment of one particular religious sect to the exclusion of all others—that, indeed, the governmental endorsement of that prayer seems relatively insignificant when compared to the governmental encroachments upon religion which were commonplace 200 years ago. To those who may subscribe to the view that because the Regents' official prayer is so brief and general there can be no danger to religious freedom in its governmental establishment, however, it may be appropriate to say in the words of James Madison, the author of the First Amendment:

[I]t is proper to take alarm at the first experiment on our liberties. . . . Who does not see that the same authority which can establish Christianity, in exclusion

of all other Religions, may establish with the same
ease any particular sect of Christians, in exclusion of
all other Sects? That the same authority which can
force a citizen to contribute three pence only of his
property for the support of any one establishment,
may force him to conform to any other establishment
in all cases whatsoever?

The judgment of the Court of Appeals of New York is re-
versed and the cause remanded for further proceedings not
inconsistent with this opinion.

Faculty-Led Public School Prayer Does Not Violate the First Amendment

Potter Stewart

An experienced judge who served on the Supreme Court from 1958 until 1981, Justice Potter Stewart (1915–1985) is remembered for his dedication to racial and gender equality and his unyielding opposition to censorship. In addition to supporting the publication of the Pentagon Papers (which opened up the U.S. government's Vietnam War policy to detailed criticism), Stewart coined what has become the most well-known judicial interpretation of obscenity: "I know it when I see it."

In the 1962 *Engel v. Vitale* case, the U.S. Supreme Court ruled that a school board's policy to begin each schoolday with a nondenominational prayer violated the First Amendment's prohibition against government establishment of religion. Only one justice disagreed with this ruling: Potter Stewart. In this dissenting opinion, Stewart explains why he disagrees with the Supreme Court's ruling and does not object to voluntary faculty-led public school prayer.

As you read, consider the following questions:
1. What defense does Stewart offer against criticism that public school prayer violates the First Amendment clause prohibiting the establishment of religion?
2. According to Stewart, what are the primary benefits of government-sanctioned prayer?

Potter Stewart, dissenting opinion, *Engel v. Vitale*, 1962.

A local school board in New York has provided that those pupils who wish to do so may join in a brief prayer at the beginning of each school day, acknowledging their dependence upon God and asking His blessing upon them and upon their parents, their teachers, and their country. The Court today decides that in permitting this brief nondenominational prayer the school board has violated the Constitution of the United States. I think this decision is wrong.

The Court does not hold, nor could it, that New York has interfered with the free exercise of anybody's religion. For the state courts have made clear that those who object to reciting the prayer must be entirely free of any compulsion to do so, including any "embarrassments and pressures." But the Court says that in permitting school children to say this simple prayer, the New York authorities have established "an official religion."

With all respect, I think the Court has misapplied a great constitutional principle. I cannot see how an "official religion" is established by letting those who want to say a prayer say it. On the contrary, I think that to deny the wish of these school children to join in reciting this prayer is to deny them the opportunity of sharing in the spiritual heritage of our Nation.

"In God We Trust"

The Court's historical review of the quarrels over the *Book of Common Prayer* in England throws no light for me on the issue before us in this case. England had then and has now an established church. Equally unenlightening, I think, is the history of the early establishment and later rejection of an official church in our own States. For we deal here not with the establishment of a state church, which would, of course, be constitutionally impermissible, but with whether school children who want to begin their day by joining in prayer must be prohibited from doing so. Moreover, I think that the Court's task, in this as in all areas of constitutional adjudication, is not responsibly aided by the uncritical invocation of metaphors like the "wall of separation," a phrase nowhere to be found in the Constitution. What is relevant to the issue here is not the history of an established church in sixteenth century England or in eighteenth century America, but the history of the religious traditions of our people, reflected in countless practices of the institutions and officials of our government.

At the opening of each day's Session of this Court we stand, while one of our officials invokes the protection of God. Since the days of John Marshall our Crier has said, "God save the United States and this Honorable Court." Both the Senate and the House of Representatives open their daily Sessions with prayer. Each of our Presidents, from George Washington to John F. Kennedy, has upon assuming his Office asked the protection and help of God.

The Court today says that the state and federal governments are without constitutional power to prescribe any particular form of words to be recited by any group of the American people on any subject touching religion. One of the stanzas of "The Star-Spangled Banner," made our National Anthem by Act of Congress in 1931, contains these verses:

> *Blest with victory and peace, may the heav'n rescued*
> *land*
> *Praise the Pow'r that hath made and preserved us a*
> *nation!*
> *Then conquer we must, when our cause it is just,*
> *And this be our motto "In God is our Trust."*

In 1954 Congress added a phrase to the Pledge of Allegiance to the Flag so that it now contains the words "one Nation under God, indivisible, with liberty and justice for all." In 1952 Congress enacted legislation calling upon the President each year to proclaim a National Day of Prayer. Since 1865 the words "IN GOD WE TRUST" have been impressed on our coins.

Countless similar examples could be listed, but there is no need to belabor the obvious. It was all summed up by this Court just ten years ago in a single sentence: "We are a religious people whose institutions presuppose a Supreme Being" (*Zorach v. Clauson*, 1952).

I do not believe that this Court, or the Congress, or the President has by the actions and practices I have mentioned established an "official religion" in violation of the Constitution. And I do not believe the State of New York has done so in this case. What each has done has been to recognize and to follow the deeply entrenched and highly cherished spiritual traditions of our Nation—traditions which come down to us from those who almost two hundred years ago avowed their "firm Reliance on the Protection of divine Providence" when they proclaimed the freedom and independence of this brave new world.

I dissent.

4

A WELL-REGULATED MILITIA

CHAPTER PREFACE

A well-regulated militia, being necessary to the security of a free state, the right of the people to keep and bear arms, shall not be infringed.

—Amendment II

From the perspective of early Americans, the Revolutionary War represented the victory of a relatively small group of civilians over one of the world's most powerful and intimidating armies. Even prior to the war, colonists resented the presence of British troops in their midst, complaining that soldiers frequently harassed the local populations. (This objection is reflected in the Third Amendment, which specifies that soldiers cannot commandeer civilian homes during peacetime.) Because of the hostility felt toward the British army, and the great success that American civilians had achieved against it, early Americans were wary of establishing a standing army of their own. Elbridge Gerry, an important figure in the early constitutional debates who would later serve as vice president in the James Madison administration, described standing armies as "the bane of liberty." He argued that one of the primary duties of the civilian militia was to prevent a national standing army from ever being formed. Nearly all males between the ages of eighteen and fifty were expected to own and maintain firearms in order to serve in the civilian militia should war arise or the government become oppressive.

As opposition to standing armies began to diminish, the U.S. Army was created and the original civilian militia became the National Guard. What did not diminish was the Second Amendment, which tied together the concepts of the well-regulated militia and the individual right to bear arms. The unclear wording of the amendment has generated a significant debate over precisely what it is supposed to guarantee.

Many gun-control advocates believe that the Second Amendment has no meaning outside of the context of the civilian militia. They argue that the right to bear arms is not a fundamental human right and only applies in cases where it contributes to a militia's collective ability to defend itself.

Others argue that the Second Amendment guarantees a basic human right to bear arms, comparable to the basic human rights to free expression and religious liberty. This view seems most consistent with the popular attitude expressed at the time of the constitutional debate: that the civilian militia would be independent from the national government and could overthrow that government should it become corrupt. "What country can preserve its liberties," Thomas Jefferson once wrote, "if its rulers are not warned from time to time that this people preserve the spirit of resistance?"

On the other hand, opponents of the human rights interpretation argue that eighteenth-century firearms were rare enough that gun control as we know it today would have been an almost inconceivable concept. Those drafting the Bill of Rights had suffered from a shortage of firearms, not a glut of them. They also had no way of predicting how firearms might evolve over the next two centuries. Would they have protected semiautomatic rifles, grenade launchers, or handguns?

In addition to the controversy over the meaning of the Second Amendment itself, there is additional debate over whether the amendment prevents state governments from passing laws that prohibit or restrict firearm ownership. Prior to the twentieth century, the Bill of Rights was only applied to federal law, not state law. In the early 1900s, however, the Supreme Court began to rule that the Fourteenth Amendment prohibited states from restricting individual rights contained in the Bill of Rights, although the Court has never made such a ruling regarding gun ownership. Supporters of the civilian militia interpretation argue that the Second Amendment was written to protect state militias from federal incursion, not to prevent state regulation. Supporters of the right-to-bear-arms interpretation contend that the Second Amendment describes an individual right, and that state laws restricting gun ownership are subsequently unconstitutional under the Fourteenth Amendment.

The right-to-bear-arms controversy is not a minor issue of judicial interpretation; it is a fundamental disagreement about what the Second Amendment is and what it was written to protect. The documents in the following chapter discuss this divisive issue.

Proposal for a Civilian Militia

George Washington

A veteran of the French and Indian War, George Washington (1732–1799) had already retired from military life and was serving quietly as a judge in Fairfax County, Virginia, when the Revolutionary War broke out in 1775. As the most experienced military officer available, he led the Continental army to an unlikely victory.

Washington faced a unique problem when the war ended in 1783: American colonists did not want a professional army, but it was clear that some means of self-defense would be necessary. He proposed a civilian militia (the "well-regulated militia" described in the Second Amendment) that would be supervised by a small number of full-time soldiers. The civilian militia would be made up of a first-response team of enthusiastic, highly trained part-time volunteers and a larger national militia that would include nearly every male citizen between the ages of eighteen and fifty. In this excerpt from his proposal, Washington describes how his militia could be organized. Although it has gone through many changes to better respond to America's military needs, the Continental Militia still exists today as the Army National Guard.

After proposing his militia, George Washington returned to his family home in Virginia, vowing to retire "under the shadow of my own vine and my own fig tree." His second retirement lasted about three years. In 1789, he became the first president of the United States.

George Washington, *The Writings of George Washington*, edited by John C. Fitzpatrick. Washington, DC: Government Printing Office, 1931–1944.

As you read, consider the following questions:
1. Washington argues that most citizens should be held responsible for bearing arms on behalf of the United States, should the need arise. In your opinion, how has the American concept of military service changed over the past two centuries?
2. According to Washington, what are the primary benefits of a national military rulebook?

Were it not totally unnecessary and superfluous to adduce arguments to prove what is conceded on all hands the Policy and expediency of resting the protection of the Country on a respectable and well established Militia, we might not only shew the propriety of the measure from our peculiar local situation, but we might have recourse to the Histories of Greece and Rome in their most virtuous and Patriotic ages to demonstrate the Utility of such Establishments. Then passing by the Mercinary Armies, which have at one time or another subverted the liberties of all-most all the Countries they have been raised to defend, we might see, with admiration, the Freedom and Independence of Switzerland supported for Centuries, in the midst of powerful and jealous neighbours, by means of a hardy and well organized Militia. We might also derive useful lessons of a similar kind from other Nations of Europe, but I believe it will be found, the *People of this Continent* are too well acquainted with the Merits of the subject to require information or example. I shall therefore proceed to point out some general outlines of their duty, and conclude this head with a few particular observations on the regulations which I conceive ought to be immediately adopted by the States at the instance and recommendation of Congress.

An Army of Citizens
It may be laid down as a primary position, and the basis of our system, that every Citizen who enjoys the protection of a free Government, owes not only a proportion of his prop-

erty, but even of his personal services to the defence of it, and consequently that the Citizens of America (with a few legal and official exceptions) from 18 to 50 Years of Age should be borne on the Militia Rolls, provided with uniform Arms, and so far accustomed to the use of them, that the Total strength of the Country might be called forth at a Short Notice on any very interesting Emergency, for these purposes they ought to be duly organized into Commands of the same formation; it is not of *very* great importance, whether the Regiments are large or small, provided a sameness prevails in the strength and composition of them and I do not know that a better establishment, than that under which the Continental Troops now are, can be adopted. They ought to be regularly Mustered and trained, and to have their Arms and Accoutrements inspected at certain appointed times, not less than once or twice in the course of every [year] but as it is obvious, amongst such a Multitude of People (who may indeed be useful for temporary service) there must be a great number,

George Washington

who from domestic Circumstances, bodily defects, natural awkwardness or disinclination, can never acquire the habits of Soldiers; but on the contrary will injure the appearance of any body of Troops to which they are attached, and as there are a sufficient proportion of able bodied young Men, between the Age of 18 and 25, who, from a natural fondness for Military parade (which passion is almost ever prevalent at that period of life) might easily be enlisted or drafted to form a Corps in every State, capable of resisting any sudden impression which might be attempted by a foreign Enemy, while the remainder of the National forces would have time to Assemble and make preparations for the Field. I would wish therefore, that the former, being considered as a *denier resort*, reserved for some great occasion, a judicious system might be adopted for forming and placing the latter on the best possible Establishment. And that while the Men of this description shall be viewed as the Van and flower of the American Forces, ever ready for Action and zealous to be employed whenever it may become necessary in the service of their Country; they should meet with such exemptions, privileges or distinctions, as might tend to keep alive a true Military pride, a nice sense of honour, and a patriotic regard for the public. Such sentiments, indeed, ought to be instilled into our Youth, with their earliest years, to be cherished and inculcated as frequently and forcibly as possible.

It is not for me to decide positively, whether it will be ultimately most interesting to the happiness and safety of the United States, to form this Class of Soldiers into a kind of Continental Militia, selecting every 10th 15th or 20th. Man from the Rolls of each State for the purpose; Organizing, Officering and Commissioning those Corps upon the same principle as is now practiced in the Continental Army. Whether it will be best to comprehend in this body, all the Men fit for service between some given Age and no others, for example between 18 and 25 or some similar description, or whether it will be preferable in every Regiment of the proposed Establishment to have one additional Company inlisted or drafted from the best Men for 3, 5, or 7 years and distinguished by the name of the additional or light Infantry Company, always to be kept complete. The Companies might then be drawn together occasionally and formed into particular Battalions or Regiments under Field Officers appointed for that Service. One or other of these plans I think will be found indispensably necessary, if we are in earnest to have an efficient force ready for Action at a moments Warning. And I cannot conceal my private sentiment, that the formation of additional, or light Companies will be most consistent with the genius of our Countrymen and perhaps in their opinion most consonant to the spirit of our Constitution.

Planning for Future War

I shall not contend for names or forms, it will be altogether essential, and it will be sufficient that perfect Uniformity should be established throughout the Continent, and pervade, as far as possible, every Corps, whether of standing Troops or Militia, and of whatever denomination they may be. To avoid the confusion of a contrary practice, and to produce the happy consequences which will attend a uniform system of Service, in case Troops from the different parts of the Continent shall ever be brought to Act together again, I would beg leave to propose, that Congress should employ some able hand, to digest a Code of Military Rules and regulations, calculated immediately for the Militia and other Troops of the United States; And as it should seem the present system, by being a little simplified, altered, and improved, might be very well adopted to the purpose; I would take the liberty of recommending, that measures should be immediately taken for the accomplishment of this interesting business, and that an Inspector General should be appointed to superintend the execution of the proposed regulations in the several States.

A Case Against Standing Armies

Mary Wollstonecraft

Mary Wollstonecraft (1759–1797) is the most widely studied woman of the eighteenth-century English Enlightenment. Her first major philosophical work, *A Vindication of the Rights of Men* (1790), responded to Edmund Burke's *Reflections on the Revolution in France* (published earlier the same year) by defending the concept of natural rights. She followed up with a second book, *A Vindication of the Rights of Woman* (1792), a general argument against the oppressive conventions of eighteenth-century society. The book gained wide notice and established Wollstonecraft's reputation as one of the most original thinkers of her time.

In this excerpt, Wollstonecraft argues that professional armies—with their emphasis on the concepts of rank and blind obedience—are contrary to the spirit of democracy. In this respect she articulates the view held by the majority of early U.S. politicians. They believed that the American Revolution, essentially a war between an organized citizens' militia of the United States and a professional standing army of Great Britain, proved the efficacy of a civilian defense force. The Second and Third Amendments were passed in large part because their supporters felt that the amendments would remove the need for, or mitigate the abuses associated with, standing armies.

Wollstonecraft died in 1797 while giving birth to her daughter (also named Mary), who would go on to write *Frankenstein* (1816).

Mary Wollstonecraft, *A Vindication of the Rights of Woman: With Strictures on Political and Moral Subjects*. London: J. Johnson, 1792.

As you read, consider the following questions:
1. According to Wollstonecraft, why is a standing army incompatible with freedom?
2. How do standing armies affect the towns in which they reside, in the author's opinion?
3. What effect does military conformity have on character development, according to Wollstonecraft?

In what does man's pre-eminence over the brute creation consist? The answer is as clear as that a half is less than the whole; in Reason.

What acquirement exalts one being above another? Virtue; we spontaneously reply.

For what purpose were the passions implanted? That man by struggling with them might attain a degree of knowledge denied to the brutes; whispers Experience.

Consequently the perfection of our nature and capability of happiness, must be estimated by the degree of reason, virtue, and knowledge, that distinguish the individual, and direct the laws which bind society: and that from the exercise of reason, knowledge and virtue naturally flow, is equally undeniable, if mankind be viewed collectively.

The rights and duties of man thus simplified, it seems almost impertinent to attempt to illustrate truths that appear so incontrovertible; yet such deeply rooted prejudices have clouded reason, and such spurious qualities have assumed the name of virtues, that it is necessary to pursue the course of reason as it has been perplexed and involved in error, by various adventitious circumstances, comparing the simple axiom with casual deviations.

Men, in general, seem to employ their reason to justify prejudices, which they have imbibed, they cannot trace how, rather than to root them out. The mind must be strong that resolutely forms its own principles; for a kind of intellectual cowardice prevails which makes many men shrink from the task, or only do it by halves. Yet the imperfect conclusions thus drawn, are frequently very plausible, because they are built on partial experience, on just, though narrow, views.

Going back to first principles, vice skulks, with all its native deformity, from close investigation; but a set of shallow reasoners are always exclaiming that these arguments prove too much, and that a measure rotten at the core may be expedient. Thus expediency is continually contrasted with simple principles, till truth is lost in a mist of words, virtue, in forms, and knowledge rendered a sounding nothing, by the specious prejudices that assume its name.

That the society is formed in the wisest manner, whose constitution is founded on the nature of man, strikes, in the abstract, every thinking being so forcibly, that it looks like presumption to endeavour to bring forward proofs; though proof must be brought, or the strong hold of prescription will never be forced by reason; yet to urge prescription as an argument to justify the depriving men (or women) of their natural rights, is one of the absurd sophisms which daily insult common sense. . . .

The Dangers of Subordination

Every profession, in which great subordination of rank constitutes its power, is highly injurious to morality.

A standing army . . . is incompatible with freedom; because subordination and rigour are the very sinews of military discipline; and despotism is necessary to give vigour to enterprizes that one will directs. A spirit inspired by romantic notions of honour, a kind of morality founded on the fashion of the age, can only be felt by a few officers, whilst the main body must be moved by command, like the waves of the sea; for the strong wind of authority pushes the crowd of subalterns forward, they scarcely know or care why, with headlong fury.

Besides, nothing can be so prejudicial to the morals of the inhabitants of country towns as the occasional residence of a set of idle superficial young men, whose only occupation is gallantry, and whose polished manners render vice more dangerous, by concealing its deformity under gay ornamental drapery. An air of fashion, which is but a badge of slavery, and proves that the soul has not a strong individual character, awes simple country people into an imitation of the vices, when they cannot catch the slippery graces, of politeness. Every corps is a chain of despots, who, submitting and tyrannizing without exercising their reason, become dead weights of vice and folly on the community. A man of rank or fortune, sure of rising by interest, has nothing to do but to pursue some extravagant freak; whilst the needy *gentleman*, who is to rise, as the phrase turns, by his merit, becomes a servile parasite or vile pander.

Sailors, the naval gentlemen, come under the same description, only their vices assume a different and a grosser cast. They are more positively indolent, when not discharging the ceremonials of their station; whilst the insignificant fluttering of soldiers may be termed active idleness. More confined to the society of men, the former acquire a fondness for humour and mischievous tricks; whilst the latter, mixing frequently with well-bred women, catch a sentimental cant.—But mind is equally out of the question, whether they indulge the horse-laugh, or polite simper. . . .

It is of great importance to observe that the character of every man is, in some degree, formed by his profession. A man of sense may only have a cast of countenance that wears off as you trace his individuality, whilst the weak, common man has scarcely ever any character, but what belongs to the body; at least, all his opinions have been so steeped in the vat consecrated by authority, that the faint spirit which the grape of his own vine yields cannot be distinguished.

The Second Amendment Protects Individual Firearm Ownership

William Rawle

William Rawle (1759–1836) was born to a Loyalist (pro-British) family in Philadelphia, Pennsylvania. When the Revolutionary War broke out, he chose to study law in England. In 1783, he returned to practice law in his home city. There he befriended Benjamin Franklin and George Washington and became known as one of the early nineteenth century's most vocal advocates for the abolition of slavery.

Rawle was also a prolific author, best known for his *View of the Constitution of the United States* (1824). In this excerpt from that book, he discusses the Second Amendment's role as a protector of the individual right to bear arms.

As you read, consider the following questions:
1. What does Rawle describe as the primary advantage of an orderly militia?
2. According to Rawle, what are the limits of the Second Amendment?

In the second article, it is declared, that a *well regulated militia is necessary to the security of a free state;* a proposition from which few will dissent. Although in actual war, the services of regular troops are confessedly more valuable; yet, while peace prevails, and in the commencement of a war before a regular force can be raised, the militia

William Rawle, *A View of the Constitution of the United States*. Philadelphia: Nicklin, 1829.

form the palladium of the country. They are ready to repel invasion, to suppress insurrection, and preserve the good order and peace of government. That they should be well regulated, is judiciously added. A disorderly militia is disgraceful to itself, and dangerous not to the enemy, but to its own country. The duty of the state government is, to adopt such regulations as will tend to make good soldiers with the least interruptions of the ordinary and useful occupations of civil life. In this all the Union has a strong and visible interest.

The corollary, from the first position, is, that *the right of the people to keep and bear arms shall not be infringed.*

A General Prohibition

The prohibition is general. No clause in the Constitution could by any rule of construction be conceived to give to congress a power to disarm the people. Such a flagitious attempt could only be made under some general pretence by a state legislature. But if in any blind pursuit of inordinate power, either should attempt it, this amendment may be appealed to as a restraint on both.

In most of the countries of Europe, this right does not seem to be denied, although it is allowed more or less sparingly, according to circumstances. In England, a country which boasts so much of its freedom, the right was secured to Protestant subjects only, on the revolution of 1688; and it is cautiously described to be that of bearing arms for their defence, "suitable to their conditions, and as allowed by law." An arbitrary code for the preservation of game in that country has long disgraced them. A very small proportion of the people being permitted to kill it, though for their own subsistence; a gun or other instrument, used for that purpose by an unqualified person, may be seized and forfeited. [Legal scholar Sir William] Blackstone, in whom we regret that we cannot always trace the expanded principles of rational liberty, observes however, on this subject, that the prevention of popular insurrections and resistance to government by disarming the people, is oftener meant than avowed, by the makers of forest and game laws.

This right ought not, however, in any government, to be abused to the disturbance of the public peace.

An assemblage of persons with arms, for an unlawful purpose, is an indictable offence, and even the carrying of arms abroad by a single individual, attended with circumstances giving just reason to fear that he purposes to make an unlawful use of them, would be sufficient cause to require him to give surety of the peace. If he refused he would be liable to imprisonment.

The Second Amendment Protects Organized State Militias

James Clark McReynolds

There are two dominant theories of the Second Amendment: the individual rights interpretation, which is based on the idea that the Second Amendment guarantees an individual right to bear arms, and the state militia interpretation, which is based on the idea that the Second Amendment is meant to protect state militias from federal intrusion.

In *U.S. v. Miller* (1939), the Supreme Court affirmed the state militia interpretation when it found that a national law restricting the ownership and transport of unregistered firearms did not violate the Second Amendment. In the following excerpt from the *U.S. v. Miller* ruling, Supreme Court justice James Clark McReynolds (1862–1946) explains that the intent of the Second Amendment was to ensure the effectiveness of state militias.

Since that time, the Supreme Court has largely steered clear of Second Amendment challenges, leaving the question of gun control to Congress, the states, and local governments. In *Quilici v. Village of Morton Grove* (1982), the Illinois Court of Appeals ruled that a city government's decision to ban the sale of handguns was constitutional. When the ruling was challenged, the Supreme Court refused to hear the case.

McReynolds served as an antitrust attorney for the U.S. government, prosecuting monopolies and "robber barons" during the early years of the twentieth century. He was appointed to the U.S. Supreme Court in 1914, and served

James Clark McReynolds, majority opinion, *United States v. Miller*, 1939.

there until 1941. During his tenure he dissented from 310 verdicts, a record at the time.

As you read, consider the following questions:
1. According to McReynolds, what was the original purpose of the Second Amendment?
2. In McReynolds's opinion, what functions are civilian militias expected to serve?

An indictment in the District Court Western District Arkansas, charged that Jack Miller and Frank Layton 'did unlawfully, knowingly, wilfully, and feloniously transport in interstate commerce from the town of Claremore in the State of Oklahoma to the town of Siloam Springs in the State of Arkansas a certain firearm, to-wit, a double barrel 12-gauge Stevens shotgun having a barrel less than 18 inches in length, bearing identification number 76230, said defendants, at the time of so transporting said firearm in interstate commerce as aforesaid, not having registered said firearm . . . and not having in their possession a stamp-affixed written order for said firearm as provided by Section 1132c, Title 26, United States Code, 26 U.S.C.A. and the regulations issued under authority of the said Act of Congress known as the "National Firearms Act" approved June 26, 1934.' . . . A duly interposed demurrer alleged: The National Firearms Act is not a revenue measure but an attempt to usurp police power reserved to the States, and is therefore unconstitutional. Also, it offends the inhibition of the Second Amendment to the Constitution, U.S.C.A.—'A well regulated Militia, being necessary to the security of a free State, the right of the people to keep and bear Arms, shall not be infringed.' The District Court held that section 11 of the Act violates the Second Amendment. . . .

In the absence of any evidence tending to show that possession or use of a 'shotgun having a barrel of less than eighteen inches in length' at this time has some reasonable relationship to the preservation or efficiency of a well regulated militia, we cannot say that the Second Amendment guarantees the right to keep and bear such an instrument. Certainly it is not within judicial notice that this weapon is any part of the ordinary military equipment or that its use could contribute to the common defense.

Militias and Standing Armies
The Constitution as originally adopted granted to the Congress power—'To provide for calling forth the Militia to execute the Laws of the Union, suppress Insurrections and repel Invasions; To provide for organizing, arming, and disciplining, the Militia, and for governing such Part of them as may be employed in the Service of the United States, reserving to the States respectively, the Appointment of the Officers, and the Authority of training the Militia according to the discipline prescribed by Congress.' With obvious purpose to assure the continuation and render possible the effectiveness of such forces the declaration and guarantee of the Second Amendment were made. It must be interpreted and applied with that end in view.

The Militia which the States were expected to maintain and train is set in contrast with Troops which they were forbidden to keep without the consent of Congress. The sentiment of the time strongly disfavored standing armies; the common view was that adequate defense of country and laws could be secured through the Militia—civilians primarily, soldiers on occasion.

The signification attributed to the term Militia appears from the debates in the Convention, the history and legislation of Colonies and States, and the writings of approved commentators. These show plainly enough that the Militia comprised all males physically capable of acting in concert for the common defense. 'A body of citizens enrolled for military discipline.' And further, that ordinarily when called for service these men were expected to appear bearing arms supplied by themselves and of the kind in common use at the time.

[Legal philosopher William] Blackstone's *Commentaries*

. . . points out 'that king Alfred first settled a national militia in this kingdom' and traces the subsequent development and use of such forces.

[Economist] Adam Smith's *Wealth of Nations* . . . contains an extended account of the Militia. It is there said: 'Men of republican principles have been jealous of a standing army as dangerous to liberty.' 'In a militia, the character of the labourer, artificer, or tradesman, predominates over that of the soldier: in a standing army, that of the soldier predominates over every other character; and in this distinction seems to consist the essential difference between those two different species of military force.'

What the Framers Had in Mind

'The American Colonies In The 17th Century,' [an article by historian Herbert L.] Osgood . . . affirms in reference to the early system of defense in New England:

> In all the colonies, as in England, the militia system was based on the principle of the assize of arms. This implied the general obligation of all adult male inhabitants to possess arms, and, with certain exceptions, to cooperate in the work of defence. The possession of arms also implied the possession of ammunition, and the authorities paid quite as much attention to the latter as to the former. A year later (1632) it was ordered that any single man who had not furnished himself with arms might be put out to service, and this became a permanent part of the legislation of the colony (Massachusetts).

The General Court of Massachusetts, January Session 1784, provided for the organization and government of the Militia. It directed that the Train Band should 'contain all able bodied men, from sixteen to forty years of age, and the Alarm List, all other men under sixty years of age. . . .' Also, 'That every non-commissioned officer and private soldier of the said militia not under the controul of parents, masters or guardians, and being of sufficient ability therefor in the judgment of the Selectmen of the town in which he shall dwell, shall equip himself, and be constantly provided with a good fire arm, &c.'

By an Act passed April 4, 1786 (Laws 1786, c. 25), the New York Legislature directed:

> That every able-bodied Male Person, being a Citizen of this State, or of any of the United States, and residing in this State (except such Persons as are herein after excepted), and who are of the Age of Sixteen, and under the Age of Forty-five Years, shall, by the Captain or commanding Officer of the Beat in which such Citizens shall reside, within four Months after the passing of this Act, be enrolled in the Company of such Beat. . . . That every Citizen so enrolled and notified, shall, within three Months thereafter, provide himself, at his own Expense, with a good Musket or Firelock, a sufficient Bayonet and Belt, a Pouch with a Box therein to contain not less than Twenty-four Cartridges suited to the Bore of his Musket or Firelock, each Cartridge containing a proper Quantity of Powder and Ball, two spare Flints, a Blanket and Knapsack. . . .

The General Assembly of Virginia, October, 1785, declared: 'The defense and safety of the commonwealth depend upon having its citizens properly armed and taught the knowledge of military duty.' It further provided for organization and control of the Militia and directed that 'All free male persons between the ages of eighteen and fifty years,' with certain exceptions, 'shall be inrolled or formed into companies.' 'There shall be a private muster of every company once in two months.'

Also that 'Every officer and soldier shall appear at his respective muster-field on the day appointed, by eleven o'clock in the forenoon, armed, equipped, and accoutred, as follows: . . . every non-commissioned officer and private with a good, clean musket carrying an ounce ball, and three feet eight inches long in the barrel, with a good bayonet and iron ramrod well fitted thereto, a cartridge box properly made, to contain and secure twenty cartridges fitted to his musket, a good knapsack and canteen, and moreover, each non-commissioned officer and private shall have at every muster one pound of good powder, and four pounds of lead, including twenty blind cartridges; and each sergeant shall have a pair of moulds fit to cast balls for their respective companies, to be purchased by the commanding officer out of the monies arising on delinquencies. Provided, That the militia of the counties westward of the Blue Ridge, and the counties below adjoining thereto, shall not be obliged to be armed with muskets, but may have good rifles with proper accoutrements, in lieu thereof. And every of the said officers, non-commissioned officers, and privates, shall constantly keep the aforesaid arms, accoutrements, and ammunition, ready to be produced whenever called for by his commanding officer. If any private shall make it appear to the satisfaction of the court hereafter to be appointed for trying delinquencies under this act that he is so poor that he cannot purchase the arms herein required, such court shall cause them to be purchased out of the money arising from delinquents.'

Most if not all of the States have adopted provisions touching the right to keep and bear arms. Differences in the language employed in these have naturally led to somewhat variant conclusions concerning the scope of the right guaranteed. But none of them seem to afford any material support for the challenged ruling of the court.

CHAPTER

5

RIGHTS OF
THE ACCUSED

CHAPTER PREFACE

The right of the people to be secure in their persons, houses, papers, and effects, against unreasonable searches and seizures, shall not be violated, and no warrants shall issue, but upon probable cause, supported by oath or affirmation, and particularly describing the place to be searched, and the persons or things to be seized.

—Amendment IV

No person . . . shall be compelled in any criminal case to be a witness against himself.

—Amendment V

Several of the rights protected by the Bill of Rights pertain to due process, the requirement that criminal suspects be treated fairly and according to established procedures. There are literally hundreds of due-process issues associated with the Bill of Rights, and many of them remain relevant and controversial today. Two of the most historically interesting due-process issues are general search warrants and voluntary confessions.

The "right of the people to be secure . . . against unreasonable searches and seizures" described in the Fourth Amendment was most probably drafted in response to the British Writs of Assistance. These writs—also known as general warrants—allowed law enforcement officers to search anywhere they chose without permission or probable cause. British law enforcement officials frequently abused the writs for personal gain and to intimidate colonists, inspiring a great deal of public resistance. When the time came to draft a bill of rights, the idea of preventing the U.S. government from ever issuing such general warrants was an appealing one.

The arrival of new technology has necessitated a reexamination of the right to be secure from unreasonable searches and seizures. When new surveillance technology became available during the twentieth century, some states gave law enforcement officers the power to use wiretapping and bugging without first obtaining a warrant. However, the Supreme Court found this practice to be roughly equivalent to the British writs and in clear violation of the Fourth Amendment.

Although the issue of general warrants has been largely settled, the Fifth Amendment's restrictions on voluntary confessions remain a controversial topic. In the case of *Miranda v. Arizona* (1966), the Supreme Court ruled that voluntary confessions cannot be used in court unless the suspect has been informed of his or her rights in advance. In his majority ruling, Justice Earl Warren pointed out that there are many subtle ways to coerce or mislead an innocent suspect into voluntarily confessing to crimes that he or she did not commit. A suspect who had been informed that he or she could remain silent and work through an attorney would be less likely to fall for interrogation tricks. In recent years many critics have argued that the Miranda protections have gone too far, protecting the innocent from intimidation but also hampering the ability of law enforcement officials to obtain confessions and convict guilty criminals.

The due-process clauses of the Bill of Rights reflect the tension between the interests of law enforcement and the rights of the accused. American legal thinkers must continue to balance the safety of the public with the basic guarantees provided to every American citizen under the Bill of Rights.

Against General Search Warrants

James Otis

During the late 1750s, illegal smuggling was extremely popular in colonial America. Concerned about the vast and increasing amount of lost tax revenue, the government of Great Britain assigned writs of assistance to all customs officials. The writs were general search warrants that allowed the bearer to legally search any residence at will. When the British government began compensating customs officials and their informants for any smuggled goods they discovered, customs officials began to abuse the previously seldom-used writs. American colonists turned to James Otis (1725–1783), an advocate-general for Great Britain's colonial Boston court, to defend them. To the surprise of many, he agreed and, as a show of solidarity with the colonists, resigned from his high-ranking office.

In February 1761, Otis argued his case before the Superior Court of Massachusetts. In this short excerpt from his speech, transcribed by future U.S. president John Adams, Otis argues that the writs of assistance are unjust and violate the most basic principles of British law. The court disagreed with Otis, and the writs of assistance were renewed.

The American colonists did not forget the writs of assistance. After the American Revolution ended, many called for the U.S. Constitution to explicitly forbid general warrants. The Fourth Amendment did just that.

As you read, consider the following questions:
1. According to Otis, what are the primary dangers of general warrants?

James Otis, address before the Superior Court of Massachusetts, February 24, 1761.

2. How does Otis distinguish between general and special warrants?

May it please your Honors: I was desired by one of the court to look into the books, and consider the question now before them concerning Writs of Assistance. I have accordingly considered it, and now appear not only in obedience to your order, but likewise in behalf of the inhabitants of this town, who have presented another petition, and out of regard to the liberties of the subject. And I take this opportunity to declare that whether under a fee or not (for in such a cause as this I despise a fee) I will to my dying day oppose, with all the powers and faculties God has given me, all such instruments of slavery on the one hand and villainy on the other as this Writ of Assistance is.

A Danger to Liberty

It appears to me the worst instrument of arbitrary power, the most destructive of English liberty and the fundamental principles of law, that ever was found in an English lawbook. I must therefore beg your Honors' patience and attention to the whole range of an argument that may perhaps appear uncommon in many things, as well as to points of learning that are more remote and unusual, that the whole tendency of my design may the more easily be perceived, the conclusions better descend, and the force of them be better felt. I shall not think much of my pains in this cause, as I engaged in it from principle.

I was solicited to argue this cause as Advocate-General; and, because I would not, I have been charged with desertion from my office. To this charge I can give a very sufficient answer. I renounced that office and I argue this cause from the same principle; and I argue it with the greater pleasure, as it is in favor of British liberty, at a time when we hear the greatest monarch upon earth declaring from his throne that he glories in the name of Briton and that the privileges of his people are dearer to him than the most valuable prerogatives of his crown; and as it is in opposition to a kind of power, the exercise of which in former periods of history cost one king of England his head and another his throne. I have taken more pains in this cause than I ever will take again, although my engaging in this and another popular cause has raised much resentment. But I think I can sincerely declare that I cheerfully submit myself to every odious name for conscience' sake; and from my soul I despise all those whose guilt, malice, or folly has made them my foes. Let the consequences be what they will, I am determined to proceed. The only principles of public conduct that are worthy of a gentleman or a man are to sacrifice estate, ease, health, and applause, and even life, to the sacred calls of his country.

These manly sentiments, in private life, make good citizens; in public life, the patriot and the hero. I do not say that, when brought to the test, I shall be invincible. I pray God I may never be brought to the melancholy trial; but, if ever I should, it will then be known how far I can reduce to practice principles which I know to be founded in truth. In the meantime I will proceed to the subject of this writ.

General and Special Warrants

Your Honors will find in the old books concerning the office of a justice of the peace precedents of general warrants to search suspected houses. But in more modern books you will find only special warrants to search such and such houses, specially named, in which the complainant has before sworn that he suspects his goods are concealed; and will find it adjudged that special warrants only are legal. In the same manner I rely on it, that the writ prayed for in this petition, being general, is illegal. It is a power that places the liberty of every man in the hands of every petty officer. I say I admit that special Writs of Assistance, to search special places, may be granted to certain persons on oath; but I deny that the writ now prayed for can be granted, for I beg leave to make some observations on the writ itself, before I proceed to other Acts of Parliament.

In the first place, the writ is universal, being directed "to all and singular justices, sheriffs, constables, and all other officers and subjects"; so that, in short, it is directed to every subject in the King's dominions. Every one with this writ may be a tyrant; if this commission be legal, a tyrant in a legal manner, also, may control, imprison, or murder any one within the realm. In the next place, it is perpetual; there is no return. A man is accountable to no person for his doings. Every man may reign secure in his petty tyranny, and spread terror and desolation around him, until the trump of the Archangel shall excite different emotions in his soul. In the third place, a person with this writ, in the daytime, may enter all houses, shops, etc., at will, and command all to assist him. Fourthly, by this writ not only deputies, etc., but even their menial servants, are allowed to lord it over us. What is this but to have the curse of Canaan with a witness on us: to be the servants of servants, the most despicable of God's creation?

Now, one of the most essential branches of English liberty is the freedom of one's house. A man's house is his castle; and whilst he is quiet, he is as well guarded as a prince in his castle. This writ, if it should be declared legal, would totally annihilate this privilege. Custom-house officers may enter our houses when they please; we are commanded to permit their entry. Their menial servants may enter, may break locks, bars, and everything in their way; and whether they break through malice or revenge, no man, no court can inquire. Bare suspicion without oath is sufficient.

This wanton exercise of this power is not a chimerical suggestion of a heated brain. I will mention some facts. Mr. Pew had one of these writs, and, when Mr. Ware succeeded him, he endorsed this writ over to Mr. Ware; so that these writs are negotiable from one officer to another; and so your Honors have no opportunity of judging the persons to whom this vast power is delegated. Another instance is this: Mr. Justice Walley had called this same Mr. Ware before him, by a constable, to answer for a breach of the Sabbath-day Acts, or that of profane swearing. As soon as he had finished, Mr. Ware asked him if he had done. He replied, "Yes." "Well then," said Mr. Ware, "I will show you a little of my power. I command you to permit me to search your house for uncustomed goods"—and went on to search the house from the garret to the cellar; and then served the constable in the same manner!

But to show another absurdity in this writ: if it should be established, I insist upon it every person, by the 14th Charles Second, has this power as well as the custom-house officers. The words are: "It shall be lawful for any person or persons authorized," etc. What a scene does this open! Every man prompted by revenge, ill-humor, or wantonness to inspect the inside of his neighbor's house, may get a Writ of Assistance. Others will ask it from self-defence; one arbitrary exertion will provoke another, until society be involved in tumult and in blood.

Electronic Surveillance and the Fourth Amendment

Tom Clark

A Texas native and veteran of World War I, Tom Clark (1899–1977) served as U.S. attorney general under President Harry Truman. In 1949 he was appointed to the U.S. Supreme Court. Although he entered the Supreme Court as a conservative who had played a role during the first years of the anti-Communist movement, over time he became known as a champion of civil rights. He is particularly well known for his opinions in Fourth Amendment cases.

In *Berger v. New York* (1967), the Supreme Court evaluated the constitutionality of Section 813-a of the New York Code of Criminal Procedures. Section 813-a granted electronic surveillance authority based solely on an "oath or affirmation of a district attorney, or of the attorney general or of an officer above the rank of sergeant of any police department." The Supreme Court declared that this code violated Fourth Amendment prohibitions against unreasonable searches and seizures. In this excerpt from his majority opinion, Clark explains the Court's reasoning.

As you read, consider the following questions:
1. What was the Supreme Court's finding in *Wong Sun v. United States*, as described by Clark?
2. According to Clark, what are the dangers of Section 813-a?

Tom Clark, majority opinion, *Berger v. New York*, 1967.

Eavesdropping is an ancient practice which at common law was condemned as a nuisance. At one time the eavesdropper listened by naked ear under the eaves of houses or their windows, or beyond their walls seeking out private discourse. The awkwardness and undignified manner of this method as well as its susceptibility to abuse was immediately recognized. Electricity, however, provided a better vehicle and with the advent of the telegraph surreptitious interception of message began. As early as 1862 California found it necessary to prohibit the practice by statute. During the Civil War General J.E.B. Stuart is reputed to have had his own eavesdropper along with him in the field whose job it was to intercept military communications of the opposing forces. Subsequently newspapers reportedly raided one another's news gathering lines to save energy, time, and money. Racing news was likewise intercepted and flashed to bettors before the official result arrived.

Wiretapping and Bugging

The telephone brought on a new and more modern eavesdropper known as the "wiretapper." Interception was made by a connection with a telephone line. This activity has been with us for three-quarters of a century. Like its cousins, wiretapping proved to be a commercial as well as a police technique. Illinois outlawed it in 1895 and in 1905 California extended its telegraph interception prohibition to the telephone. Some 50 years ago a New York legislative committee found that police, in cooperation with the telephone company, had been tapping telephone lines in New York despite an Act passed in 1895 prohibiting it. During prohibition days wiretaps were the principal source of information relied upon by the police as the basis for prosecutions. In 1934 the Congress outlawed the interception without authorization, and the divulging or publishing of the contents of wiretaps by passing 605 of the Communications Act of 1934. New York, in 1938, declared by constitutional amendment that "[t]he right of the people to be secure against unreasonable interception of telephone and telegraph communications shall not be violated," but permitted by ex parte order of the Supreme Court of the State the interception of communications on a showing of "reasonable ground to believe that evidence of crime" might be obtained.

Sophisticated electronic devices have now been developed (commonly known as "bugs") which are capable of eavesdropping on anyone in almost any given situation. They are to be distinguished from "wiretaps" which are confined to the interception of telegraphic and telephonic communications. Miniature in size (3/8" × 3/8" × 1/8")—no larger than a postage stamp—these gadgets pick up whispers within a room and broadcast them half a block away to a receiver. It is said that certain types of electronic rays beamed at walls or glass windows are capable of catching voice vibrations as they are bounced off the surfaces. Since 1940 eavesdropping has become a big business. Manufacturing concerns offer complete detection systems which automatically record voices under almost any conditions by remote control. A microphone concealed in a book, a lamp, or other unsuspected place in a room, or made into a fountain pen, tie clasp, lapel button, or cuff link increases the range of these powerful wireless transmitters to a half mile. Receivers pick up the transmission with interference-free reception on a special wave frequency. And, of late, a combination mirror transmitter has been developed which permits not only sight but voice transmission up to 300 feet. Likewise, parabolic microphones, which can overhear conversations without being placed within the premises monitored, have been developed.

As science developed these detection techniques, lawmakers, sensing the resulting invasion of individual privacy, have provided some statutory protection for the public. Seven States, California, Illinois, Maryland, Massachusetts, Nevada, New York, and Oregon, prohibit surreptitious eavesdropping by mechanical or electronic device. However, all save Illinois permit official court-ordered eavesdropping. Some 36 States prohibit wiretapping. But of these, 27 permit "authorized" interception of some type. Federal law, as we have seen, prohibits interception and divulging or publishing of the content of wiretaps without exception. In sum, it is fair to say that wiretapping on the whole is outlawed, except for permissive use by law enforcement officials in some States; while electronic eavesdropping is—save for seven States—permitted both officially and privately. And, in six of the seven States electronic eavesdropping ("bugging") is permissible on court order.

The law, though jealous of individual privacy, has not kept pace with these advances in scientific knowledge. This is not to say that individual privacy has been relegated to a second-class position for it has been held since Lord Camden's day that intrusions into it are "subversive of all the comforts of society." And the Founders so decided a quarter of a century later when they declared in the Fourth Amendment that the people had a right "to be secure in their persons, houses, papers, and effects, against unreasonable searches and seizures. . . ." Indeed, that right, they wrote, "shall not be violated, and no Warrants shall issue, but upon probable cause, supported by Oath or affirmation, and particularly describing the place to be searched, and the persons or things to be seized.". . .

Electronic Eavesdropping and the Constitution

The Court was faced with its first wiretap case in 1928, *Olmstead v. United States*. There the interception of Olmstead's telephone line was accomplished without entry upon his premises and was, therefore, found not to be proscribed by the Fourth Amendment. The basis of the decision was that the Constitution did not forbid the obtaining of evidence by wiretapping unless it involved actual unlawful entry into the house. Statements in the opinion that a conversation passing over a telephone wire cannot be said to come within the Fourth Amendment's enumeration of "persons, houses, papers, and effects" have been negated by our subsequent cases as hereinafter noted. They found "conversation" was within the Fourth Amendment's protections, and that the use of electronic devices to capture it was a "search" within the meaning of the Amendment, and we so hold. In any event, Congress soon thereafter, and some say in answer to Olmstead, specifically prohibited the interception without authorization and the divulging or publishing of the contents of telephonic communications. . . .

The first "bugging" case reached the Court in 1942 in *Goldman v. United States*. There the Court found that the use of a detectaphone placed against an office wall in order to hear private conversations in the office next door did not violate the Fourth Amendment because there was no physical trespass in connection with the relevant interception. And in *Lee v. United States* (1952), we found that since "no trespass was committed" a conversation between Lee and a federal agent, occurring in the former's laundry and electronically recorded, was not condemned by the Fourth Amendment. Thereafter in *Silverman v. United States*, the Court found "that the eavesdropping was accomplished by means of an unauthorized physical penetration into the premises occupied by the petitioners." A spike a foot long with a microphone attached to it was inserted under a baseboard into a party wall until it made contact with the heating duct that ran through the entire house occupied by Silverman, making a perfect sounding board through which the conversations in question were overheard. Significantly, the Court held that its decision did "not turn upon the technicality of a trespass upon a party wall as a matter of local law. It is based upon the reality of an actual intrusion into a constitutionally protected area."

In *Wong Sun v. United States* (1963), the Court for the first time specifically held that verbal evidence may be the fruit of official illegality under the Fourth Amendment along with the more common tangible fruits of unwarranted intrusion. It used these words:

The exclusionary rule has traditionally barred from trial physical, tangible materials obtained either dur-

ing or as a direct result of an unlawful invasion. It follows from our holding in Silverman v. United States that the Fourth Amendment may protect against the overhearing of verbal statements as well as against the more traditional seizure of "papers and effects."

And in *Lopez v. United States* (1963), the Court confirmed that it had "in the past sustained instances of 'electronic eavesdropping' against constitutional challenge, when devices have been used to enable government agents to overhear conversations which would have been beyond the reach of the human ear. . . . It has been insisted only that the electronic device not be planted by an unlawful physical invasion of a constitutionally protected area." In this case a recording of a conversation between a federal agent and the petitioner in which the latter offered the agent a bribe was admitted in evidence. Rather than constituting "eavesdropping" the Court found that the recording "was used only to obtain the most reliable evidence possible of a conversation in which the Government's own agent was a participant and which that agent was fully entitled to disclose."

Evaluating Section 813-a

We, therefore, turn to New York's statute to determine the basis of the search and seizure authorized by it upon the order of a state supreme court justice, a county judge or general sessions judge of New York County. Section 813-a authorizes the issuance of an "ex parte order for eavesdropping" upon "oath or affirmation of a district attorney, or of the attorney-general or of an officer above the rank of sergeant of any police department of the state or of any political subdivision thereof. . . ." The oath must state "that there is reasonable ground to believe that evidence of crime may be thus obtained, and particularly describing the person or persons whose communications, conversations or discussions are to be overheard or recorded and the purpose thereof, and . . . identifying the particular telephone number or telegraph line involved." The judge "may examine on oath the applicant and any other witness he may produce and shall satisfy himself of the existence of reasonable grounds for the granting of such application." The order must specify the duration of the eavesdrop—not exceeding two months unless extended—and "[a]ny such order together with the papers upon which the application was based, shall be delivered to and retained by the applicant as authority for the eavesdropping authorized therein."

While New York's statute satisfies the Fourth Amendment's requirement that a neutral and detached authority be interposed between the police and the public, the broad sweep of the statute is immediately observable. It permits the issuance of the order, or warrant for eavesdropping, upon the oath of the attorney general, the district attorney or any police officer above the rank of sergeant stating that "there is reasonable ground to believe that evidence of crime may be thus obtained. . . ." Such a requirement raises a serious probable-cause question under the Fourth Amendment. Under it warrants may only issue "but upon probable cause, supported by Oath or affirmation, and particularly describing the place to be searched, and the persons or things to be seized." Probable cause under the Fourth Amendment exists where the facts and circumstances within the affiant's knowledge, and of which he has reasonably trustworthy information, are sufficient unto themselves to warrant a man of reasonable caution to believe that an offense has been or is being committed. . . .

The Fourth Amendment commands that a warrant issue not only upon probable cause supported by oath or affirmation, but also "particularly describing the place to be searched, and the persons or things to be seized." New York's statute lacks this particularization. It merely says that a warrant may issue on reasonable ground to believe that evidence of crime may be obtained by the eavesdrop. It lays down no requirement for particularity in the warrant as to what specific crime has been or is being committed, nor "the place to be searched," or "the persons or things to be seized" as specifically required by the Fourth Amendment. The need for particularity and evidence of reliability in the showing required when judicial authorization of a search is sought is especially great in the case of eavesdropping. By its very nature eavesdropping involves an intrusion on privacy that is broad in scope. As was said in *Osborn v. United States* (1966), the "indiscriminate use of such devices in law enforcement raises grave constitutional questions under the Fourth and Fifth Amendments," and imposes "a heavier responsibility on this Court in its supervision of the fairness of procedures. . . ." There, two judges acting jointly authorized the installation of a device on the person of a prospective witness to record conversations between him and an attorney for a defendant then on trial in the United States District Court. The judicial authorization was based on an affidavit of the witness setting out in detail previous conversations between the witness and the attorney concerning the bribery of jurors in the case. The recording device was, as the Court said, authorized "under the most precise and discriminate circumstances, circumstances which fully met the 'requirement of particularity'" of the Fourth Amendment. . . .

The Court [found] that the recording, although an invasion of the privacy protected by the Fourth Amendment, was admissible because of the authorization of the judges, based upon "a detailed factual affidavit alleging the commission of a specific criminal offense directly and immediately affecting the administration of justice . . . for the narrow and particularized purpose of ascertaining the truth of the affidavit's allegations." The invasion was lawful because there was sufficient proof to obtain a search warrant to make the search for the limited purpose outlined in the order of the judges. Through these "precise and discriminate" procedures the order authorizing the use of the electronic device afforded similar protections to those that are present in the use of conventional warrants authorizing the seizure of tangible evidence. . . .

By contrast, New York's statute lays down no such "precise and discriminate" requirements. Indeed, it authorizes the "indiscriminate use" of electronic devices as specifically condemned in *Osborn*. . . . New York's broadside authorization rather than being "carefully circumscribed" so as to prevent unauthorized invasions of privacy actually permits general searches by electronic devices, the truly offensive character of which . . . [was once] known as "general warrants." The use of the latter was a motivating factor behind the Declaration of Independence. In view of the many cases commenting on the practice it is sufficient here to point out that under these "general warrants" customs officials were given blanket authority to conduct general searches for goods imported to the Colonies in violation of the tax laws of the Crown. The Fourth Amendment's requirement that a warrant "particularly describ[e] the place to be searched, and the persons or things to be seized," repudiated these general warrants and "makes general searches . . . impossible and prevents the seizure of one thing under a warrant describing another. As to what is to be taken, nothing is left to the discretion of the officer executing the warrant" (*Marron v. United States*, 1927).

We believe the statute here is equally offensive. First, as we have mentioned, eavesdropping is authorized without requiring belief that any particular offense has been or is being committed; nor that the "property" sought, the conversations, be particularly described. The purpose of the probable-cause requirement of the Fourth Amendment, to keep the state out of constitutionally protected areas until it has reason to believe that a specific crime has been or is being committed, is thereby wholly aborted. Likewise the statute's failure to describe with particularity the conversations sought gives the officer a roving commission to "seize" any and all conversations. It is true that the statute requires the naming of "the person or persons whose communications, conversations or discussions are to be overheard or recorded. . . ." But this does no more than identify the person whose constitutionally protected area is to be invaded rather than "particularly describing" the communications, conversations, or discussions to be seized. As with general warrants this leaves too much to the discretion of the officer executing the order.

Secondly, authorization of eavesdropping for a two-month period is the equivalent of a series of intrusions, searches, and seizures pursuant to a single showing of probable cause. Prompt execution is also avoided. During such a long and continuous (24 hours a day) period the conversations of any and all persons coming into the area covered by the device will be seized indiscriminately and without regard to their connection with the crime under investigation. Moreover, the statute permits, and there were authorized here, extensions of the original two-month period—presumably for two months each—on a mere showing that such extension is "in the public interest." Apparently the original grounds on which the eavesdrop order was initially issued also form the basis of the renewal. . . .

Third, the statute places no termination date on the eavesdrop once the conversation sought is seized. This is left entirely in the discretion of the officer.

Finally, the statute's procedure . . . has no requirement for notice as do conventional warrants, nor does it overcome this defect by requiring some showing of special facts. On the contrary, it permits unconsented entry without any showing of exigent circumstances. Such a showing of exigency, in order to avoid notice, would appear more important in eavesdropping, with its inherent dangers, than that required when conventional procedures of search and seizure are utilized. . . . In short, the statute's blanket grant of permission to eavesdrop is without adequate judicial supervision or protective procedures.

Voluntary Confessions and the Fifth Amendment

Earl Warren

Earl Warren (1891–1974), one of the most influential Supreme Court justices of the twentieth century, is still remembered as a major figure of the civil rights movement. Elected attorney general of California in 1938, Warren went on to serve two terms as the state's governor. He made two unsuccessful bids for national office (running for president in 1944 and for vice president in 1948) before he was nominated to the Supreme Court as chief justice in 1953. Selected by President Dwight D. Eisenhower, a fellow Republican for whom he had campaigned, Warren was initially dismissed as a political appointee with little experience in the criminal justice system. He established his relevance—and his place in history—with his majority ruling in *Brown v. Board of Education* (1953), a landmark Supreme Court case that overturned the "separate but equal" doctrine of public school segregation.

In *Miranda v. Arizona* (1966), Warren's majority opinion radically changed traditional definitions of what constitutes a proper confession. In 1963, twenty-three-year-old Ernesto Miranda was arrested on rape and kidnapping charges. A police officer lied to Miranda, claiming that he had been identified by the victim. Faced with an apparently certain guilty verdict, Miranda gave a confession. His attorney argued that the confession was essentially coerced and should never have been admitted as evidence, but the local judge disagreed and convicted Miranda. The case was appealed all the way to the U.S. Supreme Court, which ruled (in a narrow 5–4 ruling) that use of the confession as

Earl Warren, majority opinion, *Miranda v. Arizona*, 1966.

evidence violated Miranda's Fifth Amendment rights. In this excerpt from his majority opinion, Warren explains his decision.

As a result of *Miranda v. Arizona*, police are now required to inform suspects of their rights upon arrest by means of the following statement:

> You have the right to remain silent. Anything you say can and will be used against you in a court of law. You have the right to speak to an attorney, and to have an attorney present during any questioning. If you cannot afford a lawyer, one will be provided for you at government expense.

As you read, consider the following questions:
1. According to Warren, what effect might privacy have on a suspect's ability to defend himself?
2. Does Warren describe Ernesto Miranda's confession as voluntary, involuntary, or somewhere in between?

The cases before us raise questions which go to the roots of our concepts of American criminal jurisprudence: the restraints society must observe consistent with the Federal Constitution in prosecuting individuals for crime. More specifically, we deal with the admissibility of statements obtained from an individual who is subjected to custodial police interrogation and the necessity for procedures which assure that the individual is accorded his privilege under the Fifth Amendment to the Constitution not to be compelled to incriminate himself. . . .

Over 70 years ago, our predecessors on this Court eloquently stated:

> The maxim *nemo tenetur seipsum accusare* ["no one is required to incriminate himself"] had its origin in a protest against the inquisitorial and manifestly unjust methods of interrogating accused persons, which

[have] long obtained in the continental system, and, until the expulsion of the Stuarts from the British throne in 1688, and the erection of additional barriers for the protection of the people against the exercise of arbitrary power, [were] not uncommon even in England. While the admissions or confessions of the prisoner, when voluntarily and freely made, have always ranked high in the scale of incriminating evidence, if an accused person be asked to explain his apparent connection with a crime under investigation, the ease with which the questions put to him may assume an inquisitorial character, the temptation to press the witness unduly, to browbeat him if he be timid or reluctant, to push him into a corner, and to entrap him into fatal contradictions, which is so painfully evident in many of the earlier state trials, notably in those of Sir Nicholas Throckmorton, and Udal, the Puritan minister, made the system so odious as to give rise to a demand for its total abolition. The change in the English criminal procedure in that particular seems to be founded upon no statute and no judicial opinion, but upon a general and silent acquiescence of the courts in a popular demand. But, however adopted, it has become firmly embedded in English, as well as in American jurisprudence. So deeply did the iniquities of the ancient system impress themselves upon the minds of the American colonists that the States, with one accord, made a denial of the right to question an accused person a part of their fundamental law, so that a maxim, which in England was a mere rule of evidence, became clothed in this country with the impregnability of a constitutional enactment. (*Brown v. Walker*, 1896)

Our holding . . . is this: the prosecution may not use statements, whether exculpatory or inculpatory, stemming from custodial interrogation of the defendant unless it demonstrates the use of procedural safeguards effective to secure the privilege against self-incrimination. By custodial interrogation, we mean questioning initiated by law enforcement officers after a person has been taken into custody or otherwise deprived of his freedom of action in any significant way. As for the procedural safeguards to be employed, unless other fully effective means are devised to inform accused persons of their right of silence and to assure a continuous opportunity to exercise it, the following measures are required. Prior to any questioning, the person must be warned that he has a right to remain silent, that any statement he does make may be used as evidence against him, and that he has a right to the presence of an attorney, either retained or appointed. The defendant may waive effectuation of these rights, provided the waiver is made voluntarily, knowingly and intelligently. If, however, he indicates in any manner and at any stage of the process that he wishes to consult with an attorney before speaking there can be no questioning. Likewise, if the individual is alone and indicates in any manner that he does not wish to be interrogated, the police may not question him. The mere fact that he may have answered some questions or volunteered some statements on his own does not deprive him of the right to refrain from answering any further inquiries until he has consulted with an attorney and thereafter consents to be questioned.

The constitutional issue we decide in each of these cases is the admissibility of statements obtained from a defendant questioned while in custody or otherwise deprived of his freedom of action in any significant way. In each, the defendant was questioned by police officers, detectives, or a prosecuting attorney in a room in which he was cut off from the outside world. In none of these cases was the defendant given a full and effective warning of his rights at the outset of the interrogation process. In all the cases, the questioning elicited oral admissions, and in three of them, signed statements as well which were admitted at their trials. They all thus share salient features—incommunicado interrogation of individuals in a police-dominated atmosphere, resulting in self-incriminating statements without full warnings of constitutional rights.

Interrogations and Coercion

An understanding of the nature and setting of this in-custody interrogation is essential to our decisions today. The difficulty in depicting what transpires at such interrogations stems from the fact that in this country they have largely taken place incommunicado. From extensive factual studies undertaken in the early 1930's, including the famous Wickersham Report to Congress by a Presidential Commission, it is clear that police violence and the "third degree" flourished at that time. In a series of cases decided by this Court long after these studies, the police resorted to physical brutality—beating, hanging, whipping—and to sustained and protracted questioning incommunicado in order to extort confessions. The Commission on Civil Rights in 1961 found much evidence to indicate that "some policemen still resort to physical force to obtain confessions." The use of physical brutality and violence is not, unfortunately, relegated to the past or to any part of the country. Only recently in Kings County, New York, the police brutally beat, kicked and placed lighted cigarette butts on the back of a potential witness under interrogation for the purpose of securing a statement incriminating a third party.

The examples given above are undoubtedly the exception now, but they are sufficiently widespread to be the object of concern. Unless a proper limitation upon custodial interrogation is achieved—such as these decisions will advance—there can be no assurance that practices of this nature will be eradicated in the foreseeable future. The conclusion of the Wickersham Commission Report, made over 30 years ago, is still pertinent:

> To the contention that the third degree is necessary to get the facts, the reporters aptly reply in the language of the present Lord Chancellor of England (Lord Sankey): "It is not admissible to do a great right by doing a little wrong. . . . It is not sufficient to do justice by obtaining a proper result by irregular or improper means." Not only does the use of the third de-

gree involve a flagrant violation of law by the officers of the law, but it involves also the dangers of false confessions, and it tends to make police and prosecutors less zealous in the search for objective evidence. As the New York prosecutor quoted in the report said, "It is a short cut and makes the police lazy and unenterprising." Or, as another official quoted remarked: "If you use your fists, you are not so likely to use your wits." We agree with the conclusion expressed in the report, that "The third degree brutalizes the police, hardens the prisoner against society, and lowers the esteem in which the administration of justice is held by the public."

Again we stress that the modern practice of in-custody interrogation is psychologically rather than physically oriented. . . . Interrogation still takes place in privacy. Privacy results in secrecy and this in turn results in a gap in our knowledge as to what in fact goes on in the interrogation rooms. A valuable source of information about present police practices, however, may be found in various police manuals and texts which document procedures employed with success in the past, and which recommend various other effective tactics. These texts are used by law enforcement agencies themselves as guides. It should be noted that these texts professedly present the most enlightened and effective means presently used to obtain statements through custodial interrogation. By considering these texts and other data, it is possible to describe procedures observed and noted around the country.

The officers are told by the manuals that the "principal psychological factor contributing to a successful interrogation is privacy—being alone with the person under interrogation." The efficacy of this tactic has been explained as follows:

If at all practicable, the interrogation should take place in the investigator's office or at least in a room of his own choice. The subject should be deprived of every psychological advantage. In his own home he may be confident, indignant, or recalcitrant. He is more keenly aware of his rights and more reluctant to tell of his indiscretions or criminal behavior within the walls of his home. Moreover his family and other friends are nearby, their presence lending moral support. In his own office, the investigator possesses all the advantages. The atmosphere suggests the invincibility of the forces of the law. [O'Hara, *Fundamentals of Criminal Investigation* (1956)]

Interrogation Tactics

To highlight the isolation and unfamiliar surroundings, the manuals instruct the police to display an air of confidence in the suspect's guilt and from outward appearance to maintain only an interest in confirming certain details. The guilt of the subject is to be posited as a fact. The interrogator should direct his comments toward the reasons why the subject committed the act, rather than court failure by asking the subject whether he did it. Like other men, perhaps the subject has had a bad family life, had an unhappy childhood, had too much to drink, had an unrequited desire for women. The officers are instructed to minimize the moral seriousness of the offense, to cast blame on the victim or on society. These tactics are designed to put the subject in a psychological state where his story is but an elaboration of what the police purport to know already—that he is guilty. Explanations to the contrary are dismissed and discouraged.

The texts thus stress that the major qualities an interrogator should possess are patience and perseverance. One writer describes the efficacy of these characteristics in this manner:

In the preceding paragraphs emphasis has been placed on kindness and stratagems. The investigator will, however, encounter many situations where the sheer weight of his personality will be the deciding factor. Where emotional appeals and tricks are employed to no avail, he must rely on an oppressive atmosphere of dogged persistence. He must interrogate steadily and without relent, leaving the subject no prospect of surcease. He must dominate his subject and overwhelm him with his inexorable will to obtain the truth. He should interrogate for a spell of several hours pausing only for the subject's necessities in acknowledgment of the need to avoid a charge of duress that can be technically substantiated. In a serious case, the interrogation may continue for days, with the required intervals for food and sleep, but with no respite from the atmosphere of domination. It is possible in this way to induce the subject to talk without resorting to duress or coercion. The method should be used only when the guilt of the subject appears highly probable. [Ibid.]

The manuals suggest that the suspect be offered legal excuses for his actions in order to obtain an initial admission of guilt. Where there is a suspected revenge-killing, for example, the interrogator may say:

Joe, you probably didn't go out looking for this fellow with the purpose of shooting him. My guess is, however, that you expected something from him and that's why you carried a gun—for your own protection. You knew him for what he was, no good. Then when you met him he probably started using foul, abusive language and he gave some indication that he was about to pull a gun on you, and that's when you had to act to save your own life. That's about it, isn't it, Joe? [Inbau and Reed, *Criminal Interrogation and Confessions* (1962)]

Having then obtained the admission of shooting, the interrogator is advised to refer to circumstantial evidence which negates the self-defense explanation. This should enable him to secure the entire story. One text notes that "Even if he fails to do so, the inconsistency between the subject's original denial of the shooting and his present admission of at least doing the shooting will serve to deprive him of a self-defense 'out' at the time of trial."

When the techniques described above prove unavailing, the texts recommend they be alternated with a show of some hostility. One ploy often used has been termed the "friendly-unfriendly" or the "Mutt and Jeff" act:

> . . . In this technique, two agents are employed. Mutt, the relentless investigator, who knows the subject is guilty and is not going to waste any time. He's sent a dozen men away for this crime and he's going to send the subject away for the full term. Jeff, on the other hand, is obviously a kindhearted man. He has a family himself. He has a brother who was involved in a little scrape like this. He disapproves of Mutt and his tactics and will arrange to get him off the case if the subject will cooperate. He can't hold Mutt off for very long. The subject would be wise to make a quick decision. The technique is applied by having both investigators present while Mutt acts out his role. Jeff may stand by quietly and demur at some of Mutt's tactics. When Jeff makes his plea for cooperation, Mutt is not present in the room. [O'Hara, *Fundamentals of Criminal Investigation* (1956)]

Deception and Implication

The interrogators sometimes are instructed to induce a confession out of trickery. The technique here is quite effective in crimes which require identification or which run in series. In the identification situation, the interrogator may take a break in his questioning to place the subject among a group of men in a line-up. "The witness or complainant (previously coached, if necessary) studies the line-up and confidently points out the subject as the guilty party." Then the questioning resumes "as though there were now no doubt about the guilt of the subject." A variation on this technique is called the "reverse line-up":

The accused is placed in a line-up, but this time he is identified by several fictitious witnesses or victims who associated him with different offenses. It is expected that the subject will become desperate and confess to the offense under investigation in order to escape from the false accusations. [Ibid.]

The manuals also contain instructions for police on how to handle the individual who refuses to discuss the matter entirely, or who asks for an attorney or relatives. The examiner is to concede him the right to remain silent. . . . After this psychological conditioning, however, the officer is told to point out the incriminating significance of the suspect's refusal to talk:

Joe, you have a right to remain silent. That's your privilege and I'm the last person in the world who'll try to take it away from you. If that's the way you want to leave this, O.K. But let me ask you this. Suppose you were in my shoes and I were in yours and you called me in to ask me about this and I told you, 'I don't want to answer any of your questions.' You'd think I had something to hide, and you'd probably be right in thinking that. That's exactly what I'll have to think about you, and so will everybody else. So let's sit here and talk this whole thing over. [Inbau and Reed, *Criminal Interrogation and Confessions* (1962)]

Few will persist in their initial refusal to talk, it is said, if this monologue is employed correctly.

In the event that the subject wishes to speak to a relative or an attorney, the following advice is tendered:

[T]he interrogator should respond by suggesting that the subject first tell the truth to the interrogator himself rather than get anyone else involved in the matter. If the request is for an attorney, the interrogator may suggest that the subject save himself or his family the expense of any such professional service, particularly if he is innocent of the offense under investigation. The interrogator may also add, "Joe, I'm only looking for the truth, and if you're telling the truth, that's it. You can handle this by yourself." [Ibid.]

From these representative samples of interrogation techniques, the setting prescribed by the manuals and observed in practice becomes clear. In essence, it is this: To be alone with the subject is essential to prevent distraction and to deprive him of any outside support. The aura of confidence in his guilt undermines his will to resist. He merely confirms the preconceived story the police seek to have him describe. Patience and persistence, at times relentless questioning, are employed. . . . When normal procedures fail to produce the needed result, the police may resort to deceptive stratagems such as giving false legal advice. It is important to keep the subject off balance, for example, by trading on his insecurity about himself or his surroundings. The police then persuade, trick, or cajole him out of exercising his constitutional rights.

The Badge of Intimidation

Even without employing brutality, the "third degree" or the specific stratagems described above, the very fact of custodial interrogation exacts a heavy toll on individual liberty and trades on the weakness of individuals. . . . In the cases before us today, given this background, we concern ourselves primarily with this interrogation atmosphere and the evils it can bring. In *Miranda v. Arizona*, the police arrested the defendant and took him to a special interrogation room where they secured a confession. In *Vignera v. New York*, the defendant made oral admissions to the police after interrogation in the afternoon, and then signed an inculpatory statement upon being questioned by an assistant district attorney later the same evening. In *Westover v.*

United States, the defendant was handed over to the Federal Bureau of Investigation by local authorities after they had detained and interrogated him for a lengthy period, both at night and the following morning. After some two hours of questioning, the federal officers had obtained signed statements from the defendant. Lastly, in *California v. Stewart*, the local police held the defendant five days in the station and interrogated him on nine separate occasions before they secured his inculpatory statement.

In these cases, we might not find the defendants' statements to have been involuntary in traditional terms. Our concern for adequate safeguards to protect precious Fifth Amendment rights is, of course, not lessened in the slightest. In each of the cases, the defendant was thrust into an unfamiliar atmosphere and run through menacing police interrogation procedures. The potentiality for compulsion is forcefully apparent, for example, in *Miranda*, where the indigent Mexican defendant was a seriously disturbed individual with pronounced sexual fantasies, and in *Stewart*, in which the defendant was an indigent Los Angeles Negro who had dropped out of school in the sixth grade. To be sure, the records do not evince overt physical coercion or patent psychological ploys. The fact remains that in none of these cases did the officers undertake to afford appropriate safeguards at the outset of the interrogation to insure that the statements were truly the product of free choice.

It is obvious that such an interrogation environment is created for no purpose other than to subjugate the individual to the will of his examiner. This atmosphere carries its own badge of intimidation. To be sure, this is not physical intimidation, but it is equally destructive of human dignity. The current practice of incommunicado interrogation is at odds with one of our Nation's most cherished principles— that the individual may not be compelled to incriminate himself. Unless adequate protective devices are employed to dispel the compulsion inherent in custodial surroundings, no statement obtained from the defendant can truly be the product of his free choice.

Voluntary Confessions Should Always Be Admissible in Court

Antonin Scalia

A former law professor and assistant U.S. attorney general, Antonin Scalia (b. 1936) was nominated to the U.S. Supreme Court by President Ronald Reagan in 1986. He immediately established himself as an outspoken conservative who believes in the philosophy of judicial restraint—the idea that the Supreme Court should play a less active role in interpreting law. Although few regularly agree with him (Scalia is perhaps best known for his dissenting opinions), he is widely regarded as an intellectually rigorous justice who makes his decisions based on a consistent legal philosophy.

In 1966, the U.S. Supreme Court's ruling in *Miranda v. Arizona* established that voluntary confessions are not admissible in cases in which the suspect has not been informed of his or her rights (or, as many call it today, "Mirandized"). Two years later, the U.S. Congress passed Section 3501 (18 U.S.C. 3501) in response, stating that voluntary confessions are, in fact, admissible. In *U.S. v. Dickerson* (1999), the Supreme Court overruled Section 3501 and claimed that, under the Fifth Amendment, voluntary confessions are not admissible in cases in which the suspect has not been informed of his or her rights. In the following dissent, Justice Scalia argues that the *Miranda* verdict has eclipsed the Fifth Amendment itself as a standard by which voluntary confessions are judged, which he regards as an unfair restriction of congressional power by the judiciary.

Antonin Scalia, dissenting opinion, *United States v. Dickerson*, 1999.

As you read, consider the following questions:
1. In Scalia's opinion, what are the practical disadvantages of the *Miranda* ruling?
2. According to Scalia, what has the *Miranda* ruling come to symbolize?

Early in this Nation's history, this Court established the sound proposition that constitutional government in a system of separated powers requires judges to regard as inoperative any legislative act, even of Congress itself, that is "repugnant to the Constitution.". . . [This] power . . . will thus permit us, indeed require us, to "disregar[d]" §3501, a duly enacted statute governing the admissibility of evidence in the federal courts, only if it "be in opposition to the constitution"—here, assertedly, the dictates of the Fifth Amendment.

It was once possible to characterize the so-called Miranda rule as resting (however implausibly) upon the proposition that what the statute here before us [3501] permits—the admission at trial of un-Mirandized confessions—violates the Constitution. That is the fairest reading of the Miranda case itself. The Court began by announcing that the Fifth Amendment privilege against self-incrimination applied in the context of extrajudicial custodial interrogation—itself a doubtful proposition as a matter both of history and precedent. . . . Having extended the privilege into the confines of the station house, the Court liberally sprinkled throughout its sprawling 60-page opinion suggestions that, because of the compulsion inherent in custodial interrogation, the privilege was violated by any statement thus obtained that did not conform to the rules set forth in *Miranda*, or some functional equivalent. . . .

The dissenters, for their part, also understood *Miranda*'s holding to be based on the "premise . . . that pressure on the suspect must be eliminated though it be only the subtle influence of the atmosphere and surroundings.". . . ("[I]t has never been suggested, until today, that such questioning was so coercive and accused persons so lacking in hardihood that the very first response to the very first question following the commencement of custody must be conclusively presumed to be the product of an overborne will.") And at least one case decided shortly after *Miranda* explicitly confirmed the view. See *Orozco v. Texas* (1969) ("[T]he use of these admissions obtained in the absence of the required warnings was a flat violation of the Self-Incrimination Clause of the Fifth Amendment as construed in *Miranda*").

The Act of Confession

So understood, *Miranda* was objectionable for innumerable reasons, not least the fact that cases spanning more than 70 years had rejected its core premise that, absent the warnings and an effective waiver of the right to remain silent and of the (thitherto unknown) right to have an attorney present, a statement obtained pursuant to custodial interrogation was necessarily the product of compulsion. See *Crooker v. California* (1958) (confession not involuntary despite denial of access to counsel); *Cicenia v. Lagay* (1958) (same); *Powers v. United States* (1912) (lack of warnings and counsel did not render statement before United States Commisioner involuntary); *Wilson v. United States* (1896) (same). Moreover, history and precedent aside, the decision in *Miranda*, if read as an explication of what the

Antonin Scalia

Constitution requires, is preposterous. There is, for example, simply no basis in reason for concluding that a response to the very first question asked, by a suspect who already knows all of the rights described in the Miranda warning, is anything other than a volitional act. . . .

And even if one assumes that the elimination of compulsion absolutely requires informing even the most knowledgeable suspect of his right to remain silent, it cannot conceivably require the right to have counsel present. There is a world of difference, which the Court recognized under the traditional voluntariness test but ignored in *Miranda*, between compelling a suspect to incriminate himself and preventing him from foolishly doing so of his own accord. Only the latter (which is not required by the Constitution) could explain the Court's inclusion of a right to counsel and the requirement that it, too, be knowingly and intelligently waived. Counsel's presence is not required to tell the suspect that he need not speak; the interrogators can do that. The only good reason for having counsel there is that he can be counted on to advise the suspect that he should not speak. See *Watts v. Indiana* (1949) (Jackson, J., concurring in result in part and dissenting in part) ("[A]ny lawyer worth his salt will tell the suspect in no uncertain terms to make no statement to police under any circumstances").

Preventing foolish (rather than compelled) confessions is likewise the only conceivable basis for the rules (suggested in *Miranda*), that courts must exclude any confession elicited by questioning conducted, without interruption, after the suspect has indicated a desire to stand on his right to remain silent, or initiated by police after the suspect has expressed a desire to have counsel present. Nonthreatening attempts to persuade the suspect to reconsider that initial decision are not, without more, enough to render a change of heart the product of anything other than the suspect's free will. Thus, what is most remarkable about the *Miranda* decision—and what made it unacceptable as a matter of straightforward constitutional interpretation . . .—is its palpable hostility toward the act of confession per se, rather than toward what the Constitution abhors, compelled confession. See *United States v. Washington* (1977) ("[F]ar from being prohibited by the Constitution, admissions of guilt by wrongdoers, if not coerced, are inherently desirable"). The Constitution is not, unlike the *Miranda* majority, offended by a criminal's commendable qualm of conscience or fortunate fit of stupidity. . . .

Imposing Extraconstitutional Constraints

For these reasons, and others more than adequately developed in the *Miranda* dissents and in the subsequent works of the decision's many critics, any conclusion that a violation of the Miranda rules necessarily amounts to a violation of the privilege against compelled self-incrimination can claim no support in history, precedent, or common sense, and as a result would at least presumptively be worth reconsidering even at this late date. But that is unnecessary, since the Court has (thankfully) long since abandoned the notion that failure to comply with *Miranda*'s rules is itself a violation of the Constitution. . . .

Today's judgment converts *Miranda* from a milestone of judicial overreaching into the very Cheops' Pyramid (or perhaps the Sphinx would be a better analogue) of judicial arrogance. In imposing its Court-made code upon the States, the original opinion at least asserted that it was demanded by the Constitution. Today's decision does not pretend that it is—and yet still asserts the right to impose it against the will of the people's representatives in Congress. Far from believing that *stare decisis* ["let stand what is decided"] compels this result, I believe we cannot allow to remain on the books even a celebrated decision—especially a celebrated decision—that has come to stand for the proposition that the Supreme Court has power to impose extraconstitutional constraints upon Congress and the States. This is not the system that was established by the Framers, or that would be established by any sane supporter of government by the people.

CHRONOLOGY

1649–1658
The Maryland colony passes the Religious Toleration Act of 1649, granting religious freedom to all Christians. In 1654 anti-Catholic legislators overthrow the act and bar all Catholics from the colony's legislature. King Charles I overrules their decision and reinstates the Religious Toleration Act in 1658.

1663
Britain grants Rhode Island a new royal charter guaranteeing religious liberty and freedom of expression. It becomes, in effect, the first American bill of rights.

1689
The English Parliament passes a limited bill of rights, which will serve as a model for future American rights declarations.

1775–1783
During the American Revolution, colonists fight to establish their independence from Great Britain.

1776
On June 12, the Virginia Convention adopts George Mason's sixteen-point Virginia Declaration of Rights. It will influence the Declaration of Independence, approved by the Continental Congress on July 4.

1780
The Commonwealth of Massachusetts approves a thirty-point declaration of rights, which includes provisions on the right to bear arms and the quartering of soldiers.

1783

General George Washington proposes a U.S. defense force consisting largely of a well-regulated civilian militia.

1787

The Constitutional Convention meets for about four months, and the resulting U.S. Constitution is approved on September 17. Some legislators suggest incorporating a Bill of Rights into the Constitution, but are voted down. The Northwest Ordinance guarantees freedom of religion, jury trials, and a ban on cruel and unusual punishment to U.S. citizens living northwest of the Ohio River.

1789

The first ten amendments to the U.S. Constitution, referred to as the Bill of Rights, are proposed by James Madison and approved by Congress.

1798–1802

In 1798 Congress approves the three Alien and Sedition Acts, which criminalize some forms of political speech and allow the president to expel noncitizens without filing for a warrant. Two of the acts expire in 1800 and 1801, and the third is struck down by Congress in 1802.

1802

In a January letter to the Danbury Baptist Association, President Thomas Jefferson writes that the First Amendment creates "a wall of separation between church and state."

1803

In *Marbury v. Madison*, the U.S. Supreme Court establishes that it has the authority to strike down unconstitutional legislation.

1833

In *Barron v. Baltimore*, the U.S. Supreme Court rules that the Bill of Rights does not apply to state law.

1861–1865

During the American Civil War, a group of pro-slavery southern states known as the Confederate States of America rebel against the U.S. government.

1868

The Fourteenth Amendment is ratified, reserving rights to citizens on a federal level regardless of state law.

1871

The National Rifle Association (NRA) is founded. Although originally created as a hobbyist's marksmanship group, the NRA will later become the most visible organization arguing on behalf of the individual right to bear arms.

1873

Pro-censorship activist Anthony Comstock is appointed special inspector for the U.S. Postal Service. He champions rigorous new postal restrictions (referred to as the Comstock Law), and creates the Society for the Suppression of Vice.

1879

In *Reynolds v. United States*, the Supreme Court rules that laws against polygamy do not violate the First Amendment's religious free-exercise clause.

1886

In *Presser v. Illinois*, the Supreme Court rules that state laws restricting paramilitary groups do not violate the Second Amendment.

1912

Birth control advocate Margaret Sanger's article "What Every Girl Should Know" is barred by the U.S. Postal Service under the Comstock Law, primarily because it mentions sexually transmitted diseases.

1918

Congress passes the Sedition Act, which criminalizes some forms of political speech.

1919

In *U.S. v. Abrams*, the Supreme Court rules that the Sedition Act is constitutional.

1920

Concerned about the Sedition Act and other controversial World War I legislation, a group of concerned citizens create the American Civil Liberties Union (ACLU).

1921

Congress strikes down the Sedition Act of 1918, and most individuals punished under the act are granted clemency.

1933

A federal court finds that James Joyce's *Ulysses* is not obscene.

1939

In *United States v. Miller*, the Supreme Court rules that firearm registration laws do not violate the Second Amendment.

1940

Congress passes the Alien Registration Act (Smith Act), which restricts speech that advocates overthrowing the government. Although 141 people will be arrested under the act, only 29 will be successfully prosecuted.

1942

In *Chaplinsky v. New Hampshire*, the Supreme Court rules that public statements specifically intended to provoke a violent reaction—"fighting words"—are not protected by the First Amendment.

1943

In *West Virginia State Board of Education v. Barnette*, the Supreme Court rules that, under the First Amendment, public school students cannot be required to recite the Pledge of Allegiance.

1947

In *Everson v. Board of Education*, the Supreme Court rules that public school funds cannot be used to transport students to religious schools. In its ruling, it establishes what has become the standard interpretation of the First Amendment's religious establishment clause: "Neither a state nor the Federal Government . . . can pass laws which aid one religion, aid all religions, or prefer one religion over another."

1957

In *Yates v. United States*, the Supreme Court rules that enforcement of the Alien Registration Act of 1940 in cases where no subversive action has taken place violates the First Amendment.

1962

In *Engel v. Vitale*, the Supreme Court rules that, under the First Amendment, public schools cannot establish official prayers.

1966

In *Miranda v. Arizona*, the Supreme Court rules that, under the Fifth Amendment, voluntary confessions are not admissible in court unless the suspect has been informed of his or her rights in advance.

1967

In *Berger v. New York*, the Supreme Court rules that laws granting general wiretapping powers to law enforcement officers violate the Fourth Amendment.

1968

In response to widespread protests resulting from the Vietnam War, Congress passes a Federal Flag Desecration Act, making it illegal to show a lack of respect for "any flag of the United States by publicly mutilating, defacing, defiling, burning or trampling upon it."

In *Epperson v. Arkansas*, the Supreme Court rules that state laws banning the teaching of evolution are implicitly religious, and violate the First Amendment's religious establishment clause.

1970–1971

In *Welsh v. United States* (1970), the Supreme Court rules that those who are philosophically opposed to war may claim conscientious objector status and avoid the draft under the First Amendment's free-exercise clause, regardless of whether they belong to an organized religion.

In *Gillette v. United States* (1971), the Court rules that conscientious objector status can only be granted in cases where the draftee opposes all wars—not just specific ones.

1980

In *Stone v. Graham*, the Supreme Court rules that posting the Ten Commandments in a public school classroom violates the First Amendment's religious establishment clause.

1982

In *Quilici v. Morton Grove*, a federal appeals court rules that a city law banning the sale of handguns does not violate the Second Amendment. The Supreme Court declines to hear the case.

1983

In *Marsh v. Chambers*, the Supreme Court rules that voluntary state legislative prayer ceremonies do not violate the First Amendment's religious establishment clause because they are voluntary and do not involve coercion.

1988

In *Employment Division v. Smith*, the Supreme Court rules that laws banning the distribution of peyote—a hallucinogenic drug used in some American Indian religious ceremonies—do not violate the First Amendment's religious free-exercise clause.

1989–1990

In *Texas v. Johnson* (1989), the Supreme Court rules that laws banning desecration of the U.S. flag violate the First Amendment. Congress quickly rewords the Federal Flag Desecration Act of 1968 in an attempt to conform to the Court's ruling, but the Court finds in *United States v. Eichman* (1990) that the new revision is also unconstitutional. In an effort to circumvent the Court, some in Congress propose a new constitutional amendment banning flag desecration but fail to secure enough votes.

1993

Congress passes the Religious Freedom Restoration Act, which attempts to circumvent some Supreme Court rulings by establishing a new constitutional standard for interpreting the First Amendment's free-exercise clause.

1997

The Supreme Court strikes down the Religious Freedom Restoration Act of 1993 on grounds that it violates constitutional safeguards by interfering with the judiciary branch's power to review legislation.

1998

In *ACLU v. Reno*, the Supreme Court rules that a federal law banning "indecent" material on the Internet violates the First Amendment.

2003

In *Virginia v. Black*, the Supreme Court rules that laws restricting cross burning as a form of intimidation do not violate the First Amendment.

FOR FURTHER RESEARCH

General Works on the U.S. Bill of Rights

Akhil Reed Amar, *The Bill of Rights: Creation and Reconstruction*. New Haven, CT: Yale University Press, 2000.

Bernard Bailyn, ed., *The Debate on the Constitution: Federalist and Antifederalist Speeches, Articles, and Letters During the Struggle Over Ratification*. 2 vols. New York: Library of America, 1993.

Neil H. Cogan, ed., *The Complete Bill of Rights: The Drafts, Debates, Sources, and Origins*. New York: Oxford University Press, 1997.

Saul Cornell, *The Other Founders: Anti-Federalism and the Dissenting Tradition in America, 1788–1828*. Chapel Hill: University of North Carolina Press, 1999.

Michael Kent Curtis, *No State Shall Abridge: The Fourteenth Amendment and the Bill of Rights*. Durham, NC: Duke University Press, 1990.

Gordon Lloyd and Margie Lloyd, eds., *The Essential Bill of Rights: Original Arguments and Founding Documents*. Lanham, MD: University Press of America, 1998.

Linda R. Monk, *The Bill of Rights: A User's Guide*. 3rd ed. Alexandria, VA: Close Up Foundation, 2000.

William E. Nelson, *Marbury v. Madison: The Origins and Legacy of Judicial Review*. Lawrence: University Press of Kansas, 2000.

James F. Simon, *What Kind of Nation: Thomas Jefferson, John Marshall, and the Epic Struggle to Create a United States*. New York: Simon & Schuster, 2002.

Gary Zacharias and Jared Zacharias, eds., *The Bill of Rights*. San Diego, CA: Greenhaven Press, 2002.

Freedom of Speech, Press, and Assembly

Joel M. Gora, David Goldberger, Gary M. Stern, and Morton H. Halperin, *The Right to Protest: The Basic ACLU Guide to Free Expression.* Carbondale: Southern Illinois University Press, 1991.

Robert Hargreaves, *The First Freedom: A History of Free Speech.* Gloucestershire, England: Sutton Publishing, 2003.

Nat Hentoff, *First Freedom: The Tumultuous History of Free Speech in America.* New York: Delacorte Press, 1988.

Sheila Seuss Kennedy, ed., *Free Expression in America: A Documentary History.* Westport, CT: Greenwood Press, 1999.

Robert W.T. Martin, *The Free and Open Press: The Founding of American Democratic Press Liberty, 1640–1800.* New York: New York University Press, 2001.

Richard Polenberg, *Fighting Faiths: The Abrams Case, the Supreme Court, and Free Speech.* Ithaca, NY: Cornell University Press, 1999.

Religious Establishment and Freedom of Religion

Daniel L. Dreisbach, *Thomas Jefferson and the Wall of Separation Between Church and State.* New York: New York University Press, 2002.

Edwin Gaustad and Leigh Schmidt, *The Religious History of America.* Rev. ed. San Francisco: HarperSanFrancisco, 2002.

Frank Lambert, *Founding Fathers and the Place of Religion in America.* Princeton, NJ: Princeton University Press, 2003.

Barry W. Lynn, Marc D. Stern, and Oliver S. Thomas, *The Right to Religious Liberty: The Basic ACLU Guide to Religious Rights*. Carbondale: Southern Illinois University Press, 1995.

John J. Patrick and Gerald P. Long, eds., *Constitutional Debates on Freedom of Religion: A Documentary History*. Westport, CT: Greenwood Press, 1999.

Frank S. Ravitch, *School Prayer and Discrimination: The Civil Rights of Religious Minorities and Dissenters*. Boston: Northeastern University Press, 2001.

The Second Amendment and the Right to Bear Arms

Saul Cornell and Ronald E. Shalhope, eds., *Whose Right to Bear Arms Did the Second Amendment Protect?* New York: St. Martin's Press, 2000.

Michael D. Doubler and John W. Listman Jr., *The National Guard: An Illustrated History of America's Citizen Soldier*. Dulles, VA: Brassey's, 2003.

H. Richard Uviller and William G. Merkel, *The Militia and the Right to Arms, or, How the Second Amendment Fell Silent*. Durham, NC: Duke University Press, 2003.

David E. Young, ed., *The Origins of the Second Amendment: A Documentary History*. 2nd ed. Ontonagon, MI: Golden Oak Books, 2001.

Rights of the Accused and Convicted

Jeffrey Abramson, *We the Jury: The Jury System and the Ideal of Democracy*. New York: Basic Books, 1995.

Liva Baker, *Miranda: Crime, Law, and Politics*. New York: Macmillan, 1985.

Lawrence M. Friedman, *Crime and Punishment in American History*. New York: Basic Books, 1994.

Hayley R. Mitchell, ed., *The Complete History of the Death Penalty.* San Diego, CA: Greenhaven Press, 2000.

Other Books of Interest

Alexander Hamilton, James Madison, and John Jay, *The Federalist Papers.* Eds. Charles R. Kesler and Clinton Rossiter. New York: Mentor Books, 1999.

Thomas Jefferson, *Writings.* Ed. Merrill D. Peterson. New York: Library of America, 1984.

Ralph Ketcham, ed., *The Anti-Federalist Papers and the Constitutional Convention Debates.* New York: Mentor Books, 1996.

Isaac Kramnick, ed., *The Portable Enlightenment Reader.* New York: Penguin, 1995.

Walter Lacqueur and Barry Rubin, eds., *The Human Rights Reader.* Rev. ed. New York: Penguin, 1990.

Thomas Paine, *Collected Writings.* Ed. Eric Foner. New York: Library of America, 1995.

Roy Porter, *The Creation of the Modern World: The Untold Story of the British Enlightenment.* New York: W.W. Norton, 2001.

Websites

American Civil Liberties Union, www.aclu.org. Founded in 1920, this controversial organization supports a broad libertarian interpretation of the Bill of Rights by filing or funding civil liberties lawsuits. The website includes an extensive news section dealing with recent controversies pertaining to the Bill of Rights.

Bill of Rights Institute, www.billofrightsinstitute.org. This organization is dedicated to educating high school students and teachers about the origins of, and controversies pertaining to, the U.S. Bill of Rights. The website includes relevant news, free curriculum material, and discussions of landmark Supreme Court cases.

First Amendment Center, www.firstamendmentcenter.org. This website, hosted with support from Vanderbilt University, addresses legal matters arising from concerns about the constitutional guarantees provided by the First Amendment.

Founders' Constitution, http://press-pubs.uchicago.edu/founders. This website includes primary-source material pertaining to every section of the Constitution.

National Rifle Association, www.nra.org. Originally founded in 1871 as a sportsmen's organization, the NRA is the largest and most vocal organization dedicated to the individual right to bear arms. The website includes an extensive news section dealing with recent Second Amendment controversies, as well as an extensive history section.

Religious Freedom Page, http://religiousfreedom.lib.virginia.edu. This website provides information on religious freedom and tolerance, with emphasis on the United States.

INDEX

religious persecution in,
138
Writs of Assistance of,
168, 170
English Bill of Rights
(1689), 12, 13, 24, 25–28
*Essay on the First Principle
of Government* (Priestley),
123
executive branch, 59
explicit rights, 38–40

"Federal Farmer," 36
Federalist Papers, The, 49
Federalists, 14–15, 22–23
Fifth Amendment, 168
voluntary confessions and,
185–201
firearms
interpretation of Second
Amendment and,
147–48
Second Amendment
protects the right to
own, 158–60
First Amendment
criticism of government
and
is protected, 81–88
restrictions on, 73–80
should be permitted,
67–72
freedom of expression
guaranteed by, 65–66
nationalism and, 102–104
obscenity and censorship
and, 89–97
pledge of allegiance and,
98–104

public school prayer does
not violate, 141–44
con, 131–40
religious freedom
protected in, 106–107,
138–39
sedition and, 76–78
flag, saluting, 98–104
Fourteenth Amendment,
16, 17–19, 147–48
Fourth Amendment, 19
electronic surveillance
and, 175–84
general search warrants
and, 168–69
freedom of expression
criticism of government
and, 67–72
First Amendment
protects, 81–88
restrictions on, 73–80
First Amendment
guarantee of, 65–66
intent and, 84–86
right to, 85–86
freedom of religion. *See*
religious freedom
freedom of the press,
46–48, 52–53, 65
punishment for slander
and, 76–80
see also freedom of
expression
free speech, 85–86
see also freedom of
expression
French Revolution (1789),
116, 124